LEBANON

TITLES IN THE MODERN NATIONS OF THE WORLD SERIES INCLUDE:

Afghanistan
Australia
Austria
Brazil
Cambodia
Canada
China
Cuba
Czech Republic
England
Ethiopia
France
Germany
Greece
Haiti
Hungary
India
Iran
Iraq
Ireland
Israel
Italy
Japan

Jordan
Kenya
Lebanon
Mexico
Nigeria
Norway
Pakistan
Peru
Poland
Russia
Saudi Arabia
Scotland
Somalia
South Africa
South Korea
Spain
Sweden
Switzerland
Taiwan
Thailand
Turkey
United States
Vietnam

LEBANON

BY LINDA HUTCHISON

LUCENT BOOKS ®

THOMSON

★

GALE ™

San Diego • Detroit • New York • San Francisco • Cleveland • New Haven, Conn. • Waterville, Maine • London • Munich

THOMSON

★

™

GALE

Dedication
I would like to thank my sons, Raul and Erik Rathmann, for their
love and support; my mother, sister, and friends for their encour-
agement; and my editor, Lauri Friedman, for her vision in helping
shape this book.

On cover: Rooftops in Tripoli

© 2003 by Lucent Books. Lucent Books is an imprint of The Gale Group, Inc.,
a division of Thomson Learning, Inc.

Lucent Books® and Thomson Learning™ are trademarks used herein under license.

For more information, contact
Lucent Books
27500 Drake Rd.
Farmington Hills, MI 48331-3535
Or you can visit our Internet site at http://www.gale.com

LIBRARY OF CONGRESS CATALOGING-IN-PUBLICATION DATA

Hutchison, Linda
    Lebanon / by Linda Hutchison.
        p. cm. — (Modern nations of the world)
    Summary: Presents information on the history, geography, people, culture, and
    contemporary issues of the country of Lebanon.
    Includes bibliographical references and index.
        ISBN 1-59018-116-6
    1. Lebanon—Juvenile Literature. [1. Lebanon.] I. Title. II. Series.
        DS80.H88 2003
        956.92—dc21

                                                                                    2002011024

Printed in the United States of America

CONTENTS

INTRODUCTION

LEBANON: CAUGHT IN THE CROSSFIRE

Once known as a beautiful Mediterranean resort, the country of Lebanon became a devastated war zone in less than a generation. Caught in the middle of conflict between Israel and the Palestinians, and between its own Christians and Muslims, Lebanon became a terrible example of the ravages of war and the never-ending turmoil in the Middle East. "Bombed out like Beirut" became a common expression to describe anything destroyed as completely as Lebanon's capital city.

Just twenty years earlier, in the years following its independence in 1944, Lebanon was flourishing. Known for its unique combination of Eastern and Western culture, it was the most sophisticated of all Arab countries. Tourists were welcomed to sample this diversity of culture and geography, to sunbathe at the seaside, or to ski in the mountains. A major financial and commercial center, Beirut was called "the Paris of the Middle East."

The land that is now Lebanon has been attracting a variety of people for at least seven thousand years. From the Egyptians to the French, at least twelve different civilizations have invaded, settled in, and shaped Lebanon in some way. Many religious sects, both Christian and Muslim, have also sought refuge in Lebanon. This made Lebanon unlike any other country in the Middle East. British Journalist Robert Fisk, who has been based in Beirut for twenty-five years, describes it as follows:

> When I arrived in Beirut from Europe, I felt the oppressive, damp heat, saw the unkempt palm trees and smelt the Arabic coffee, the fruit stalls, and the over-spiced meat. It was the beginning of the Orient. And when I flew back to Beirut from Iran, I could pick up the British papers, ask for a gin and tonic at any bar, choose a French, Italian or German restaurant for dinner. It was the beginning of the West. All things to all people, the Lebanese rarely question their own identity.[1]

Underneath this appearance of sophisticated tolerance, all was not well, however. The divisions between people remained as pronounced as the gorges, mountains, and valleys cutting through the country. Resentment and conflicts intensified as groups wrestled for control of the country. As many as twenty different groups formed armed militias, including the Palestinians, who had fled Israel and were living in refugee camps. The Israeli army invaded. The Syrian army moved in. Multinational forces, including American, Italian, and French, arrived. Caught in this crossfire, Lebanon was not able to withstand the civil war that followed.

Today the people of Lebanon are rebuilding their country. As they dig down through the rubble, they are uncovering the remains of ancient cities founded by people who were sophisticated and prosperous. Although it will take many years of hard work, the Lebanese must also discover a modern identity, one that reaches across and embraces all its cultures, churches, and mosques. In doing so, Lebanon can once again bring peace and prosperity to its own beautiful land, and to the countries that surround it.

Lebanese children ride scooters in downtown Beirut. The city was recently rebuilt after being destroyed during the civil war.

1

BIGGER THAN ITS BORDERS

Lebanon is a land of paradoxes, where things seem one way but are actually another. For example, it is one of the smallest countries in the world, yet one of the biggest in terms of geographical and cultural diversity. It is one of the newer countries in the world, yet one of the oldest lands historically.

Lebanon occupies a rectangular slice of land 25 to 35 miles wide by 135 miles long on the eastern edge of the Mediterranean Sea. Within those approximately four thousand square miles—slightly less than the area of the state of Connecticut,

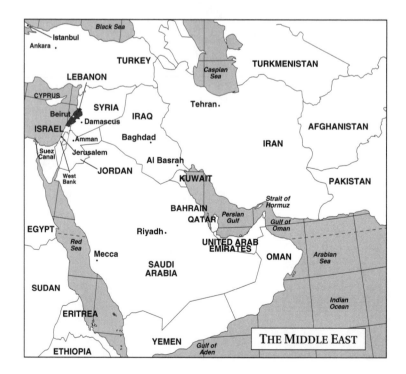

THE MIDDLE EAST

or one-fortieth the size of the state of California—lies an incredible diversity of coastal plain, mountains, rivers, and valleys. It is this topography that has attracted diverse cultures for thousands of years, each shaping Lebanon's cultural and political makeup in some way.

Lebanon is bordered on the north and east by Syria, on the south by Israel, and on the west by the Mediterranean Sea. Its major regions include the coastal plain, the mountains, and the Bekaa Valley.

THE COASTAL PLAIN

The coastal plain area runs the length of the country: 135 miles from the Syrian border in the north to the Israeli border in the south. It varies in width, from between one and eight miles. The northern half of the coastline is rocky; the southern half of the coastline is flatter, with sandy beaches. The coastal plain is scored with deep gorges, called *wadis,* formed by streams that flow from the mountains in spring and summer.

The climate along the coast is temperate, with humid, warm summers and mild winters. There are about three hundred sunny days and thirty-six inches of rain a year. It was in this area as long ago as 10,000 B.C. that humans first began to cultivate grains and to form communities. Called Canaanites, and later Phoenicians, these earliest inhabitants eventually developed city-states where the land was fertile and the coast provided natural harbors.

Today most of Lebanon's major coastal cities are built on these ancient sites. Archaeologists are still uncovering relics from the early Phoenician civilization as well as from ones that followed, including Egyptian, Greek, and Roman. Outside these cities on the coastal plain, the land is still used for farming; it is covered with groves of fruit trees, including oranges, lemons, bananas, olives, and grapes.

THE MOUNTAINS

Two major mountain ranges run parallel to each other down the length of Lebanon: the Lebanon Mountains on the west and the Anti-Lebanon mountain range on the east. It is from these mountains that the country derives its name, from the Semitic root *laban,* meaning white, or *labnan,* meaning to be white. Most likely, white refers to the

THE CEDARS OF LEBANON

The cedar tree (*Cedrus libani*) is native to the eastern Mediterranean. It is an evergreen conifer with a large trunk and a wide crown, and grows up to eighty feet. Considered a symbol of strength, it is the national emblem of Lebanon. It appears on the Lebanese flag, on a field of white, symbolizing a desire for peace. Above and below the white field are red stripes, symbolizing the self-sacrifice needed for independence.

The cedar trees and forests of Lebanon have been famous since before biblical times. Thousands of years ago, the Phoenicians cut down the trees and used them to build their ships which they sailed throughout the Mediterranean and down the coast of Africa. The wood was thought to repel insects and the resin from the wood to ease toothaches. They traded the wood with the Egyptians and the Hebrews.

The Egyptians, who had no trees in the Nile Valley, used the cedar wood to build furniture, funeral barges, and coffins. When the pharaoh Tutankhamen's tomb was discovered in 1922, it contained furniture made from the cedar trees of Lebanon. In the tenth century B.C., King Solomon of the Hebrews built his palace in Jerusalem out of cedar wood.

Unfortunately, what were once vast forests covering the mountains have been cut down to small groves, covering less than 5 percent (and some say 3 percent) of the country. The largest groves are currently protected in the Chouf Cedar Reserve, where some of the trees are thought to be two thousand years old.

Several environmental organizations are working to save existing groves of cedars and to plant new ones. In addition to being cut down, many of the trees suffer from malnutrition, disease, and pollution, and from being carved into by visitors. Since the cedars are slow growing, it will take years for the replanting to make a difference.

snow that covers the mountains in the winter. The Arabic name for Lebanon is *Lubnan*.

LEBANON MOUNTAINS

Rising sharply from the sea in the north, the Lebanon Mountains follow the coastline south, veering inland where the coastal plain widens. The highest peak is Qurnet al-Sauda which towers at 11,020 feet in the north near the city of Tripoli.

The climate in the mountains is an alpine one, with fresh breezes in the summer and heavy snow in the winter. It has been a popular resort area since Roman times. In the summer, visitors arrive to escape the hot humid air on the coast, and in the winter, they fill the many ski resorts.

At one time, the mountains were covered with forests, especially with the native cedar tree, the national emblem of Lebanon. Now so many have been cut down that less than 5 percent of the country has trees. Those remaining in protected groves include varieties of cedar, pine, juniper, and oak. Many of the Lebanese who live in the mountains have carved out stone terraces and filled them with earth to grow vegetables. They use the lower slopes of the mountains for olive groves. They share the mountains with many wild animals: deer, polecats, hedgehogs, hare, the gray wolf, the gazelle (almost extinct), and the hyrax, a unique animal that looks like a large rodent with hooves but is really related to the elephant.

The Lebanon Mountains end at the mouth of the Litani River southeast of Beirut, where they are called the Chouf Mountains. "The Chouf," as the area is called, is a mixture of small villages and wild beauty. Full of rivers and canyons, it is a popular hiking destination and the location of the Chouf Cedar Reserve, the largest natural protected area in Lebanon.

CITY OF THE SUN

The town of Baalbek in the Bekaa Valley seems to have been built for celebration. The early Canaanites were the first to erect a temple there for their god Baal, lord of the sky. The Greeks called Baalbek *Heliopolis,* meaning City of the Sun.

The Romans turned the town into a resort and erected temples to their gods Jupiter, Bacchus, and Venus. The construction took about three hundred years to complete, from the first to the fourth century A.D. It was the Roman Empire's last testament to pagan worship (the worship of more than one god) before adopting Christianity.

In the centuries that followed, Christians and Arabs moved in, building churches, mosques, and fortresses. The Roman temples remain, however, the most spectacular on view anywhere in the world.

In 1956 they became a place of celebration again, the site of the yearly International Festival. Held against the backdrop of the temples, the festival has included performers from Lebanon and around the world such as American jazz greats Duke Ellington, Miles Davis, and Dizzy Gillespie; singers Ella Fitzgerald and Joan Baez; dancer Rudolf Nureyev; British rock star Sting; and Spanish guitarist Paco de Lucia. The festival was suspended in 1976, overshadowed by civil war, but true to its origins, resumed again in 1997.

The Romans erected this temple in Baalbek to honor their god of wine, Bacchus.

Covering 5 percent of the total area of Lebanon, it includes six cedar forests, with some trees thought to be two thousand years old.

ANTI-LEBANON MOUNTAIN RANGE

To the east of the Lebanon Mountains, across the Bekaa Valley, rises the Anti-Lebanon mountain range. These mountains run down the eastern edge of the country, straddling the border between Lebanon and Syria. They extend into Syria in the north and into Israel in the south.

Sheer and arid, they support little vegetation. Their highest peak—at 9,232 feet—is Mount Hermon, said to be the site where the body of Jesus reportedly rose from the dead. The Phoenicians believed that Mount Hermon was the home of their gods, including Baal, lord of the sky. Several historical sites dating back to the Byzantine and Crusader eras are located in the southern part of these mountains. With magnificent views in every direction—west to the sea, south to Israel, east to Syria, and north to the mountains—they were a natural site for forts and castles. For more than one thousand years, every civilization to invade Lebanon has fought here, including the Palestinian guerillas and the Israelis in the recent civil war.

BEKAA VALLEY

Between these two mountain ranges, in the northern half of Lebanon, lies the Bekaa Valley. The valley is a plateau approximately seventy-five miles long and from five to ten miles wide. The Romans called it Coele-Syria, or hollow Syria, because it was a corridor between the Syrian desert and the sea to the west. They also used it for growing grains. Today, the valley is Lebanon's main agricultural area, with most crops grown on farms of about twelve acres. Major crops include wheat, potatoes, tomatoes, citrus fruit, apples, grapes, olives, tobacco, cotton, and sunflowers (for oil and soap). There are also several wineries throughout the valley, a growing business. The oldest is the Ksara Winery near the resort town of Zahle, on the site of what was once a medieval fortress.

Sheltered by the surrounding mountains, the valley is drier than the coastal plain, with less than ten inches of rain a year. Aside from the crops which are irrigated by the rivers, only wild herbs and shrubs grow here; there are no trees. Summers are dry and hot and winters cold, frosty, and windy. The marshes in the valley attract many migrating birds, including flamingos, pelicans, ducks, herons, storks, and eagles.

Until recent years the valley was a big source of illegal crops for the drug trade: poppies (for opium) and cannabis (for marijuana and hashish). After Lebanon's civil war the government made the farmers replace the illegal crops with tomatoes,

The Deir Qannoubin monastery is one of many built into the rocky sides of the Qadisha Valley.

potatoes, tobacco, and grain. This was effective in stopping the drug trade, but also caused the farmers to lose much income.

SMALLER VALLEYS

Tucked into the western edges of the Lebanon Mountains are two smaller valleys: the Qadisha Valley and the Adonis Valley. In the north, under Mt. Qurnet al-Sauda, is the Qadisha Valley. It has been considered a holy place for centuries, attracting religious minorities who have built churches and monasteries into its rocky walls. Maronite Christians settled here in the seventh century and are still its major inhabitants. The Qadisha Valley includes Lebanon's oldest ski resort—The Cedars—as well as the town of Bcharre, the birthplace of Lebanon's most famous writer, Kahlil Gibran.

Farther south lies the Adonis Valley, a mountain gorge cut by the Adonis River. At the head of the river is the Afqa Grotto, a sacred place where, according to various Phoenician, Egyptian, and Greek legends, Adonis either died or had his first kiss. (Adonis was a handsome youth killed by a wild boar and brought back to life each spring for Aphrodite, the goddess of love and fertility.) For centuries this river valley has been a place of pilgrimage; shrines dot the landscape and Lebanese families often picnic there.

HOWLING DOG RIVER

A few miles north of Beirut the mouth of the Dog River opens into the sea. A deep gorge surrounded by high land, it was almost impossible to cross before the Arabs built a bridge in the fourteenth century A.D. Armies since the Egyptians had to slow down and cross the river one soldier at a time, making them vulnerable to attack. After crossing, many of these armies left stone plaques as markers on the sides of the cliffs. Twenty of these are still visible today, with inscriptions in Latin, Greek, Arabic, French, and English. The oldest shows Pharaoh Ramses II of Egypt (1292–1225 B.C.). Others include engravings by Nebuchadrezzar II of Egypt (sixth century B.C.), Roman emperor Marcus Aurelius (A.D. 198–217), and several left in the twentieth century: the British in World War I, the French in World War II, and militia fighters in the civil war.

Today a modern bridge and tunnel cross the river, which flows only in the springtime. Its legendary past lives on in the plaques and in its name: Nahr al-Kalb (River of the Dog). In Phoenician times a statue of the god Anubis (a dog's head on a human body) stood where the river plunges into deep caverns, thought to be the entrance to the underworld. Supposedly the howling of the dog could be heard far away and warned off invaders. Most likely, it was the wind howling through the river's rocky gorges and caverns.

The most spectacular of these caverns, and the source of the river, is the Jeita Grotto, located about a mile inland. Discovered in 1836 by an American hunter, the grotto is now a popular tourist site with one of the world's most spectacular formations of stalactites and stalagmites and regular sound and light shows. During the civil war the caves were used to store ammunition. In 1958 a huge upper cavern was discovered. Big enough to seat one thousand people, it carries sound well and is used for musical concerts. The lower caverns are viewable only by boat and not at all in the winter when the water level rises too high.

RIVERS

The Bekaa Valley is irrigated by Lebanon's two major rivers: the Orontes River in the north and the Litani River in the south. The Orontes River originates north of Baalbek and flows 250 miles north through Syria and west into southern Turkey where it enters the Mediterranean. It is filled with water wheels and used mostly for irrigation, especially in Syria. In northern Lebanon, some of the river's adjoining marshes have been drained and are used for farming. There are also trout farms and hiking areas with caves and waterfalls.

The Litani River originates south of Baalbek and flows ninety miles south, then west through the Lebanon Mountains, emptying into the Mediterranean north of Tyre. It is the only river in the Middle East that does not cross a national border. In 1959 it was dammed at the southern end of the valley, forming Lake Qaraaoun, the site of a bird sanctuary and several restaurants. The dam provides water to the driest parts of the southern Bekaa Valley and, through a tunnel, to the coastal plain. Most of Lebanon's cities are located on this coastal plain.

BEIRUT

Lebanon is the most urbanized of the Arab countries, with 90 percent of its population living in cities. About half of these—1.5 million—live in Beirut, the capital city. The country's mix of people is closely reflected in that of the city: about 50 percent Sunni Muslim, 20 percent Shiite Muslim, and 30 percent Christian (mostly Maronite, but some Greek Catholics and Armenians).

The city is built on a promontory, with hills in the east, cliffs on the north side, and beaches in the south. Many of the beaches are now closed to the public, covered with garbage or walled off by private developers erecting high-rise apartments and hotels. The streets are jammed with smog-making cars because there is no public transportation. Like Lebanon,

A Lebanese man dives into the sea near Beirut. Nearly half of the country's population lives in the capital city.

Beirut is full of contrasts: rich and poor, old and new, Eastern and Western. In a *Smithsonian* magazine article, "Beirut Rises from the Ashes," journalist Richard Covington describes these contrasts along the C0orniche, an oceanfront walkway that runs around the edge of the city:

> Along the Corniche's broad pedestrian walkway, teen-agers on Rollerblades zigzag around unflappable ven-dors on bicycle carts hawking roast corn and sesame pocket bread dangling from metal racks. Skimpily clad joggers pant past women wrapped in hejabs [veils]. Nonchalantly crossing their polished Italian loafers, businessmen taking a break stretch out in folding chairs and take languorous puffs from tall water pipes, an old Arab custom making a rousing comeback. Boys dive off rocks slick with algae as fishermen cast their lines into the blue-green sea rolling with foam.[2]

During the civil war, from 1975 to 1990, about a million people left Beirut when fighting between Muslim and Christian militias and between the Israelis and the Palestinians al-most destroyed it. The city was divided into two sectors: the Christians on the east and the Muslims on the west, leaving a bombed-out uninhabitable strip of land in the middle.

Since the warring groups either left or put down their arms, the city is gradually coming to life again, intent on reunifying and restoring its image as the cultural capital of the Arab world. A major business center and seaport, Beirut is a hub for most of Lebanon's imports and exports, and for trans-portation whether by sea, rail, road, or air. Lebanese are mov-ing into Beirut seeking better opportunites to make a living.

TRIPOLI

The administrative capital of Northern Lebanon, Tripoli is Lebanon's second largest city, with a population of 350,000. It was originally three cities, named from the Greek *tri* (three) and *poli* (cities). Now it consists of two parts: the port district of El Mina on a small peninsula, and the city proper about two miles inland. A small river—the Nahr Abu Ali (Qadisha)—cuts through the city into the sea.

Tripoli has been an important trading center since Phoenician times. It prospered during the Middle Ages un-der the Muslims who built many open-air markets called *souks.* These are still well preserved today. In the eighteenth century Tripoli was known for its soap making. This is being revived to cater to the modern interest in aromatherapy. Tripoli's other industries include tobacco cultivation, sponge fishing, chocolate making, and oil refining.

Tripoli suffered some damage from the civil war, but not as much as Beirut and the south. The residents are primarily Sunni Muslims.

JUBAYL (BYBLOS)

Once the capital of the Phoenician empire, Byblos—now Jubayl—is thought to be the oldest continuously occupied city in the world. Tombs and temples the Phoenicians built into the city's rock walls in the twelfth century B.C. are still visible today.

The name Byblos is derived from the Greek word *bublos*, meaning papyrus. The Egyptians often stopped here on their way to Greece with papyrus (sheets of paper made from the papyrus plant in the Nile Valley) and to trade the papyrus for cedar wood. The word "bible" also comes from this same source. A collection of papyrus sheets is *biblion* (book) and a collection of books is *biblia* (bible).

In the twelfth century A.D., the crusaders built a castle here from huge stone blocks thought to be taken from earlier Roman ruins. Named after St. John the Baptist, it was the first crusader castle to be built in the eastern Mediterranean. About fifty years after it was built, it was badly damaged in an earthquake and fortified with extra columns and side supports. Arab designs were added in the eighteenth century.

Today Jubayl has become one of Lebanon's most popular tourist destinations, known for its beautiful stone buildings with red tile roofs. Its medieval *souks* (markets) have been restored and filled with shops. Mostly, however, it remains a small fishing port where residents and visitors sit in the quiet harbor enjoying the sunsets.

Lebanon may be one of the world's smallest countries, but it has one of the largest histories. Both its location in the world as a strategic link between Asia, Europe, and Africa, and its beautiful land, which shelters diverse groups of people, have had a profound influence on this history. They will continue to do so in the years to come as Lebanon plays an important role in the events of the Middle East.

The Diverse People of Lebanon

More than any other country in the Middle East, Lebanon is a land of colorful contrasts and diversity. Seacoast cities sit next to rural farms and squatter settlements. Mountain resorts nestle next door to traditional villages. These many contrasts are just as evident in the Lebanese people themselves. Like parts of a colorful mosaic, they stand out distinctly from one another and yet are fashioned and fit into the larger picture of Lebanon.

Lebanon is the only Arab country where more than twenty recognized religious sects have lived side by side for centuries. About 35 percent of the country's sects are based on Christianity and 65 percent are based on Islam. Every adult in Lebanon carries an identification card that identifies him or her as either a Christian or a Muslim. Most Lebanese Christians are either Maronites or Melchites. Lebanese Muslims are primarily Sunnis, Shiites, or Druze. These groups have played the biggest part in shaping Lebanon as a country.

Sunni Muslims

Sunni Muslims consider themselves to be in the mainstream sect of Islam, which continues the religion as it was originally defined by the prophet Muhammad (A.D. 570–632). The name Sunni comes from Sunna, written rules of conduct which, like the Koran (Islam's holy book), guide Muslim behavior. It is the oldest and largest Muslim sect. More than 80 percent of Muslims around the world are Sunnis.

In Lebanon the Sunnis are no longer the majority Muslim sect. Although they do make up about 22 percent of Lebanon's population, they have been outnumbered in

ISLAM

Islam is based on the teachings of the prophet Muhammad and means "submission to God's will." Its followers are called Muslims. Muhammad was born around A.D. 570 in Mecca, Arabia. In about A.D. 610 he began receiving a series of revelations he attributed to God. Eventually these were written down and they became known as the Koran, Islam's holy book. Koran—also spelled Qur'an—means "recitation." Between A.D. 613 and 622 Muhammad slowly gained followers (and enemies) as he preached his beliefs. Eventually, with an army of ten thousand, he conquered his birthplace of Mecca, where he demolished the pagan idols and established the worship of Allah as the one God.

The prophet Muhammad established the Islamic faith in the early seventh century.

Muhammad died in A.D. 632. Within twenty-five years of his death, his successors—called caliphs, or companions of Muhammad—had conquered adjoining lands and brought Islam to Egypt, Palestine, Syria, Lebanon, Iran, Iraq, and Afghanistan.

Islam's beliefs are based on the Five Pillars:

- *Shahada*: believing that "There is no God but Allah, and Mohammed is his prophet."

- *Salat*: praying five times a day facing Mecca.

- *Zakat*: giving to the poor.

- *Sawn*: fasting during the month of Ramadan.

- *Hajj*: making a pilgrimage to Mecca during one's lifetime.

Muslims recognize many other prophets besides Muhammad, including Abraham, Noah, Moses, and Jesus, but they do not believe, as Christians do, that Jesus was the son of God. There are also several different sects of Muslims that have evolved over the years.

Lebanon in the last forty years by the Shiite Muslims, who have a higher birthrate. For several hundred years, however, the Sunnis enjoyed a privileged position in Lebanon's history. Since most of them were merchants and traders from the interior of Syria, Egypt, and North Africa, they settled in the business centers of the coastal towns and cities like Beirut, Tripoli, and Sidon. They prospered economically and managed to get along well with the ruling Arab dynasties, whether based in Damascus, Baghdad, or Cairo. They helped these rulers fight off the invading crusaders from Europe between A.D. 1095 and 1291. For approximately seven hundred years after the Crusades, during the Mamluk and Ottoman Empires, the Sunnis enjoyed a golden age in Lebanon. They persecuted and even converted many Shiites and Druze. They were rewarded by the Ottomans for being such loyal citizens and tended to identify more with a universal Muslim state rather than the idea of a separate country like Lebanon. Although this attitude served them well under strong rulers, it also prevented them from

Sunni Muslims pray at a Lebanese mosque. Sunnism is the oldest and largest Muslim sect.

developing self-reliance and an interest in their own political power. As a result, they had a hard time adjusting when Lebanon became a country in 1943 and were outmaneuvered by the Maronites, Druze, and Shiites for positions of power. By law, however, the country's prime minister must be a Sunni Muslim.

Today the Sunnis in Lebanon remain concentrated in the cities. With a lower birthrate (4.3 children per family) than other groups, and better jobs, they are better off economically. The Palestinians who live in twelve refugee camps in Lebanon are also Sunnis, but they are not well off economically or politically.

SHIITE MUSLIMS

Lebanon's largest and fastest-growing Muslim sect is Shiite, with 35 percent of the population and a birthrate of about five children per family.

Worldwide, Shiite Muslims make up only about 15 percent of the Muslim population, although they are the majority sects in Iraq and Iran. They began to break away from mainstream Islam almost as soon as Muhammad died in A.D. 632, believing that Muhammad wanted his cousin and son-in-law Ali to succeed him as caliph. Other Muslims did not agree, and it was twenty-four years before Ali became caliph. He was murdered only five years later. This inflamed the beliefs of his followers, who began to call themselves Shia, followers of Ali. In the following centuries, Shiites gathered many more supporters, became organized, and eventually dominated the state religion in Egypt and Persia (now Iran). During those years, the Shiites moved into almost every part of Lebanon and were protected by Shiite rulers in Damascus, Cairo, and Baghdad.

Unlike the Sunni Muslims who were merchants and traders, the Shiites were peasants, drawn to the rural farming areas outside the cities. Although generous, hospitable, and rebellious, they were not as well educated or connected to the outside world as the Sunnis. They lacked strong leadership and did little to help in the fight against the crusaders. As a result, they lost protection and were persecuted by the Sunnis under the Mamluks and Ottomans. They became even more secluded and moved away from most of the coastal towns except Tyre. Today, they make up the majority

of the farmers in the south and in the Bekaa Valley. In the last century many have migrated north into the sprawling suburbs south of Beirut nicknamed "The Belt of Misery." In recent years, more Shiites have moved upward economically, becoming part of the middle class or even the wealthier upper class. By law, the speaker of the parliament must be a Shiite Muslim.

Druze women of the Chouf Mountains gather together. Although the Druze comprise a small percentage of the population, they play an influential role in Lebanon's politics.

THE DRUZE

The smallest and yet most distinctive Muslim sect in Lebanon is Druze. Even though the Druze make up only about 7 percent of the population, they have been a powerful political force in Lebanese politics. They live mainly in the mountainous areas southeast of Beirut known as the Chouf and have their own unique dialect. Secretive in their beliefs, the Druze allow only a select few to worship, which they do in ordinary buildings rather than mosques. In order to avoid persecution in their early years, they developed secret formulas for recognizing one another, stopped trying to convert outsiders, and even adopted other religions if surrounded by them.

The Druze sect began to form after a Shiite Egyptian caliph al-Hakim declared himself God incarnate in 1016. Several missionaries took up his cause, including Muhammed al-Daraziy (from which the word Druze comes). However, both al-Daraziy and the caliph suddenly and mysteriously disappeared. Most other sects of Muslims believe that al-Hakim died, but the Druze believe that he will return to the world and bring a golden age to true believers. The Druze follow seven principles: (1) love of truth, (2) taking care of one another, (3) renouncing all other religions, (4) avoiding the demon and all wrongdoers, (5) accepting divine unity in humanity, (6) accepting all of al-Hakim's acts, (7) acting in total accordance to al-Hakim's will. They also believe in reincarnation.

Rebellious, hardy, and warlike, the Druze were driven from Egypt and settled in the mountainous areas of Lebanon. During the Crusades, they fought with the Sunnis to repel the invading European Christians and were rewarded by rulers in the following centuries. Solitary and reserved, with a tightly

ARABS

Although the people of Lebanon are divided into many religious sects, they almost all belong to one ethnic group: the Arabs. According to Insight Guides' *Syria and Lebanon* travel writers, the Arabs in Lebanon are similar to Arabs in other countries, yet also reflect Lebanon's amazing diversity:

> Sit outside a café in Damascus, Beirut, or one of the region's other cities and you will be struck by the variety of features passing by, from the palest milky-white skin with blue or green eyes to the darkest shade of brown skin and eyes with raven-black hair. The Bedu, with their long faces and prominent noses and chins, are clearly related to Arabs of the Arabian peninsula. People of the towns may have Hittite, Aramean, Philistine, Mesopotamian, Phoenician, Greek, Roman, Persian, Arab, Turk or European characteristics, but the large majority of them can also be ethnically defined as Arabs.

> In the biblical sense, "Arabs" were nomads who inhabited the deserts of northern and central Arabia. From the 7th century onwards they conquered a vast empire which, over many centuries, underwent "arabisation." Even today, there are many similarities between Arab countries all over the world, from North Africa to the Middle East and the Arabian Gulf.

knit social structure, the Druze also are self-reliant, well organized, tolerant, and able to adapt to changing circumstances.
Although not as numerous as the Sunnis or Shiites, they have
played an important part in Lebanon's politics and have been
granted several government positions. The current Minister of
the Displaced is a Druze.

MARONITE CHRISTIANS

The largest Christian sect in Lebanon is Maronite and represents about 20 percent of the population. About 60 percent
of the world's Maronites live in Lebanon. The Maronite sect
began to form in the early fifth century in northeast Syria,
based on the teachings of a hermit named Maron (now St.
Maron). Considered heretics because of their views on Jesus'
nature, the Maronites were driven out of Syria by both Christians and the invading Muslim Arabs in the seventh century.

Like the Druze, they settled in the Lebanon Mountains.
During the Crusades (A.D. 1095–1291), the Maronites supported the Catholic European invaders who were trying to
reclaim the Middle East from the Muslims. In the twelfth
century, they realigned themselves with the Catholic
Church in Rome, becoming what is known as Uniate or
Eastern Rite Catholics.

Following the Crusades, Maronite leaders lost power and
became little more than tax collectors for the Muslim Mamluks and Ottomans. This made them very unpopular with
both the peasants and the clergy, who came from peasant
backgrounds. Eventually they worked with the clergy to
establish monasteries and schools that helped educate
people, including those in surrounding Muslim and Druze
communities. Like the Druze and the Shiites, the Maronites
were rebellious, hardy, and self-reliant. More outspoken,
adventurous, and enterprising than the Druze, the Maronites excelled economically and culturally. By the seventeenth and eighteenth centuries, they became the most
widespread community in Lebanon, many migrating south
and into the cities. More than any other sect in Lebanon,
they became interested in the idea of Lebanon as a distinct
country and attracted the attention and support of other
Catholics in Europe, especially the French. A strong
Catholic nation, France declared itself the protector of the
Maronites in 1648. When the French took over the area

from the Ottomans after World War I, it was the Maronites who benefited most from the new government. By law, the Lebanese president must be a Maronite Christian.

At that time, Maronites made up more than half the population, but they are now outnumbered by the Sunni and Shiite Muslims. Many have left the country. They still have the highest standard of living and the lowest birthrate (3.5 children per family).

EARLY CHRISTIANITY IN LEBANON

Christianity is based on the teachings of Jesus and his disciples. Approximately one hundred years after his death, a substantial group of followers began to break away from Judaism and consider Jesus as the Messiah or savior, the liberator of humankind. By A.D. 380 Christianity became the official religion of the Roman Empire. This empire stretched from what is now England and Spain in the west to Armenia and Assyria in the east. By A.D. 395 the empire split in two, with Rome as the capital of the western part and Byzantium (what is now Istanbul, Turkey) as the capital of the eastern part. The eastern Roman Empire, or Byzantine Empire, which included what is now Syria and Lebanon, became more powerful than Rome, better able to fight off barbarian tribes that invaded from the north for several hundred years. During this time, many new Christian churches formed in the Middle East with their own languages and rites. These included the Maronites and the Melchites, who formed in northern Syria and moved south into the mountains of Lebanon to avoid persecution.

Along with these new churches came many differences in opinion about basic teachings and practices. Church leaders met regularly to try to resolve these differences. One conflict concerned the nature of Jesus as the Messiah: Was he divine, or human, or both? At first, most Christians believed that he was completely divine, that he had one divine nature and will, or intent. This belief became known as Monophysitism. Others began to believe that he had separate human and divine natures and wills, which became the official position of the Church at the Council of Chalcedon (near Istanbul) in A.D. 351. This alienated many Eastern Christians who preferred to believe that Jesus was completely divine. Some even converted to Islam. Eventually, in A.D. 1054 many of the Eastern churches broke away completely, forming the Eastern Orthodox branch of Christianity. In the following centuries, some of these Eastern churches realigned themselves with Roman Catholicism and accepted the Pope. These became known as Eastern Rite or Uniate churches, who acknowledge the Pope but practice their own rites in their own languages. There are several of these in Lebanon. The two largest are the Maronites and the Melchites (Greek Catholics).

MELCHITES

The Melchites (Greek Catholics and Greek Orthodox) make up about 15 percent of Lebanon's population. Like the Maronites, the sect developed in the fifth century when Greek immigrants settled in the Orontes River Valley of northern Syria. Traditional Christian Catholics, they practiced their own rites in Greek. Often following the Maronites, they began moving into Lebanon in the seventh century. They usually settled in the larger mountain towns and in the coastal cities, where they were surrounded by Sunnis.

In 1054 the Melchites became part of the Eastern Orthodox branch of Christianity which separated from the Roman Catholic Church. In 1724 many Melchites realigned themselves with the Pope and the Roman Catholics. These Melchites became known as Greek Catholics who, like the Maronites, are Uniate Catholics. Those Melchites who did not realign themselves with the Pope and remained part of the Eastern Orthodox branch are today called Greek Orthodox.

Throughout their history, most Melchites have been traders and artisans rather than peasants. Their names reflect their

Maronite Christians crowd about a Lebanese Cardinal. Practitioners of this sect enjoy Lebanon's highest standard of living.

trades: Haddad (smith), Lahham (butcher), Sayigh (gold-
smith), Najjar (carpenter), and Hayik (weaver). Enterprising,
with little interest in politics, they adapted well and thrived.
Today many Melchites live in the resort town of Zahle. According to historian Kamal Salibi, "the Greek Orthodox and
Greek Catholics of Lebanon continue to exhibit the traditional
complaisance and resourcefulness of their Melchite prede-
cessors. Politically shy, they still excel in those fields where
there is little government interference, and are economically
and culturally the most active communities in the country."[3]

For several hundred years before Lebanon became independent, these religious sects lived peacefully side by side.
According to Salibi, "Each sect managed its own internal affairs independently of the others, took a fierce pride in its
separate identity, and jealously guarded its rights. Custom
regulated polite relationships between the different groups
and prescribed a friendly manner in which ordinary differences could be settled."[4]

Even though Lebanon was not yet a nation, it did stand
out as a distinct community of sects bound by a social con-
tract which held together until the 1700s. When the Turkish
Ottoman rulers began to lose their grip on Lebanon, the
pieces of the mosaic began to come unglued and a new picture began to form.

A Link Between Empires

As a distinct country, Lebanon first appeared on maps of the world about sixty years ago. As an ancient land, however, it has been an important part of world history for thousands of years—first as the birthplace of civilization, and then as a link between the surrounding civilizations of Africa, Asia, and Europe.

Historians refer to this arc of land from Egypt in the west to Iran in the east as the Fertile Crescent or the Cradle of Civilization. It was here that humans who lived in tribes and survived as hunter-gatherers began to grow, harvest, and store edible grains and to tame and raise several animals, including dogs, pigs, sheep, goats, cows, and horses. Along the coastal plain of the Eastern Mediterranean, they settled into small villages where they lived in round huts with crushed limestone floors. As they invented tools of rock, bone, and metal, they could harvest more crops (such as peas, lentils, fruit, nuts, and olives), grow flax for cloth fiber, make beer and wine, and cut down trees for building. Their population and villages grew, evolving over the centuries into small cities with elected officials. About 4000 B.C. they began to work with metal, to make glass and pottery, and to build ships and navigate them.

Eventually the area became known as Canaan, possibly referring to the grandson of Noah described in the Old Testament. It is not known for certain if the Canaanites originated in the Fertile Crescent or if they were one of the many Semitic tribes that migrated north from the Arabian peninsula or from other parts of Asia. Their language was closely related to Hebrew, Assyrian, Aramaic, Ethiopic, and Arabic. They began calling their snow- and limestone-covered mountains a variation of *laban* (white) or *labnan* (to be white), the origin of the name Lebanon.

The Canaanites established a series of city-states along the coast, from Byblos in the north to Sidon and Tyre in the south. Most of these cities were built in two parts, with a harbor on a promontory or island and an inland area separated by a garden. By about 2800 B.C. they were exporting cedar wood, olive oil, and wine to Egypt, their Fertile Crescent neighbor to the southwest. The Canaanites excelled as sailors and sea merchants and were often used by the Egyptians as navigators. They were not soldiers, however, and not strongly united, and so were vulnerable to invasion by surrounding tribes and growing empires.

By about 1500 B.C. the Egyptians had begun to push their empire farther north and east in the Fertile Crescent. They incorporated Canaan and nearby Palestine and Syria into their empire but left administration to local princes. Between the twelfth and ninth centuries B.C. the Canaanites flourished and came to be called Phoenicians by the Greeks because of a purple dye (*phoinikes)* they extracted from murices (a type of sea mussel) and sold. They established colonies in North Africa, Spain, France, and England and sailed around Africa. They invented the first alphabet based

The captain of a supply ship (center) addresses a crew of Canaanites in this ancient wooden model. The Canaanites were one of the first groups of people to settle in what is now called Lebanon.

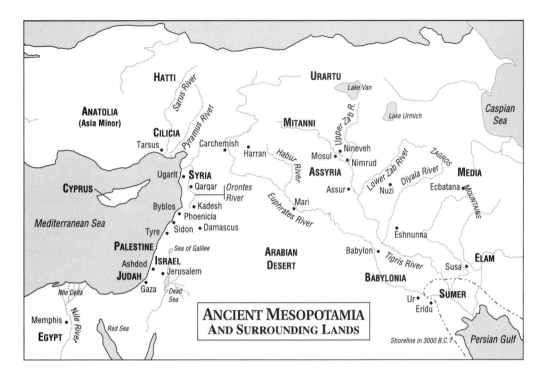

ANCIENT MESOPOTAMIA
AND SURROUNDING LANDS

on sounds (phonetic) which was to become the basis of the Roman alphabet used in the West today. About 1000 B.C. the domestication of the camel opened up new trade routes between the coast and the civilizations to the east. It was there in the Mesopotamia Valley that other empires, such as the Assyrians, the Babylonians, and the Persians began to compete for these trade routes and the valuable Phoenician knowledge of and access to the sea.

The Assyrians (not related to the Syrians) were a fierce war-like people who had developed their fighting skills defending their land in the open plains of the north Mesopotamia Valley. Like the Egyptians, they used the Phoenician cedar wood in their buildings and palaces. Between 887 and 627 B.C. they launched a series of invasions across the Syrian desert to the coast and down into Egypt, where they killed tens of thousands of people. Despised for their barbaric cruelty and excessive taxation, they were never able to fully control their territories, where people revolted constantly.

Soon they were replaced by the Babylonians from the southern part of the Mesopotamia Valley. Formerly known as Sumerians, they also were ferocious fighters. In 573 B.C. they captured Tyre after a thirteen-year siege. The Babylonians placed greater emphasis on cultural achievements than the Assyrians, but their hold on Phoenician cities ended when the Persians from north of the Euphrates River (now Iran) invaded in 539 B.C., led by Cyrus. At the time, they were seen as liberators and Phoenicia became one of the most prosperous provinces under the Persian Empire. No longer the successful sea traders they had been centuries earlier, they still had a powerful navy which supported the Persians during their wars with Greece from 490 to 449 B.C. In 346 B.C. the residents of Sidon revolted against high taxes. The Persians retaliated by burning Sidon to the ground and killing forty thousand people. The culture of Phoenicia began fading with the empires of Egypt and the Mesopotamia Valley. Other civilizations in southern Europe were now to land on the shores of what would become Lebanon and to change its people forever.

THE GREEKS

The first invaders were the Greeks, led by their new young king, Alexander the Great of Macedonia. Only twenty-three years old, he set east from Greece with a massive army. In 332 B.C. he reached the Phoenician city of Tyre whose citizens fought back behind their walled island. For seven months Alexander attacked the city, building a causeway to the island and erecting two towers to climb over the walls. He executed seven thousand citizens and sold another thirty thousand into slavery, then rebuilt Tyre as a Greek fortress.

Under the Greeks, Phoenicia was ruled as part of Palestine and Egypt and gradually absorbed much of the Greek culture. This included new architecture, new laws and customs, and a love of artistic accomplishment and philosophical inquiry. Although the Phoenicians continued to speak their own language, the Greeks refined the Phoenician alphabet, adding vowels.

The Greek Empire eventually reached east into Persia, Afghanistan, and India and south into Egypt. In all, Alexander founded seventy cities. The empire was never strongly unified, however. In its later years, it absorbed elements of the Eastern cultures it had conquered, leaving behind the mixture of East and West that has shaped Lebanon. In the meantime, Rome, another great Western empire, was expanding.

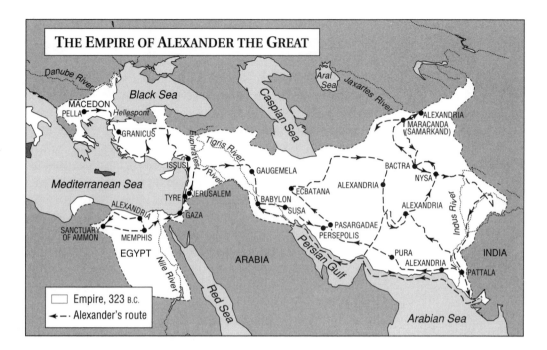

THE EMPIRE OF ALEXANDER THE GREAT

Danube River
Black Sea
MACEDON
PELLA
Hellespont
GRANICUS
Caspian Sea
Aral Sea
Jaxartes River
ALEXANDRIA
MARACANDA (SAMARKAND)
Tigris River
Euphrates River
ISSUS
GAUGEMELA
BACTRA
NYSA
Mediterranean Sea
ECBATANA
ALEXANDRIA
TYRE
JERUSALEM
BABYLON
ALEXANDRIA
Indus River
GAZA
SUSA
ALEXANDRIA
SANCTUARY OF AMMON
MEMPHIS
PASARGADAE
PERSEPOLIS
PURA
ALEXANDRIA
INDIA
EGYPT
Nile River
ARABIA
Persian Gulf
PATTALA
Red Sea
Arabian Sea

☐ Empire, 323 B.C.
◄--- Alexander's route

THE ROMANS

The Romans had been building a dynasty in Italy since the sixth century B.C. and were well aware of the military and commercial advantages of Phoenicia. In 64 B.C. they invaded. Under the Romans for the next several hundred years, Phoenicians continued to prosper, selling their famous purple dye, pottery, glass, cedar wood, perfume, jewelry, wine, and fruit. Huge warehouses in their harbors stored products from Syria, India, and Persia. The Romans governed the coastal cities, the mountains, and the desert to the east as one province they called Syria and granted everyone Roman citizenship. Berytus (Beirut) became the most important city in the province with a famous school of law under Herod the Great.

The Romans were magnificent planners and builders. As the inventors of concrete, they covered their entire empire with paved roads, bridges, temples, and palaces, many still visible today. It was along these roads, some in present-day Lebanon, that Jesus of Nazareth and his disciples Peter and Paul began teaching the beginnings of what was to become a new religion, Christianity. Within three hundred years it was accepted by the majority of people in the empire and was declared the official religion.

In A.D. 395 the Roman emperor Constantine established a new capital in the eastern part of the empire in Byzantium, renaming it Constantinople (present-day Istanbul, Turkey). This divided the empire into two parts. The western part with Rome as its capital began to decline as Europe went through a period of barbarian invasions and what was later called the Dark Ages. The eastern part of the empire, however, which came to be known as the Byzantine Empire, flourished for many more centuries, more successful at fighting off barbarian tribes than its western half. It included Syria and the old Phoenician cities. A mixture of Greek, Christian, and Eastern culture, it was a bridge between the ancient and the modern world. Across the bridge and into this mixture arrived the tribes of people from the Arabian Peninsula to the south.

THE ARABS AND ISLAM

The Arabs had already started moving north into the area of Syria and Palestine when the prophet Muhammad was born in Mecca, about A.D. 570. After the growth of his religion, Islam, and his death in A.D. 632, the Arabs moved even more rapidly into surrounding areas, driven by a desire to spread their religious beliefs and culture. They invaded the coastal

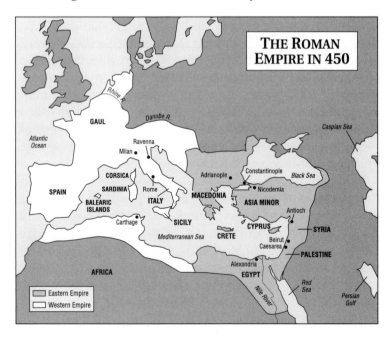

cities of what is now Lebanon in A.D. 643 and defeated the local Byzantine rulers. By 660 they had established the seat of their new empire inland in Damascus, in present-day Syria, where they felt less vulnerable to invasion. They divided the region into five provinces. For approximately one hundred years the area was governed by a family called the Umayyads. During this time the coastal cities and Mediterranean commerce went into a decline. A desert people, the Arabs were not adept at sea trade, commerce, or farming.

In A.D. 750 another Arab Muslim dynasty came into power, the Abbasids. They moved the capital of their Arab empire east to Baghdad, in present-day Iraq. Although they remained a dynasty for almost five hundred years, their central governing power weakened after about A.D. 820 as local princes or tribal chiefs and other Arab dynasties in Egypt, Persia, and Turkey jostled for leadership. The economy revived; shipping and trading increased in the seaports, especially Tyre and Tripoli, as the Arabs exported local textiles, ceramics, and glass to other parts of their empire. There was a renewed interest in science, philosophy, literature. Although the local people used Arabic for writing, they resisted learning to speak it, instead continuing to speak Aramaic and Syriac into the 1600s.

RELIGIOUS DIVISIONS AND CRUSADES

The majority of Arabs who arrived in the eastern Mediterranean region were Sunni Muslims. The Christians they encountered were Maronites, Greek Catholics, and Greek Orthodox. In the years following the birth and spread of Islam and Christianity, sects began to form based on different interpretations of basic beliefs. These included the Maronite Christians and the Shiite and Druze Muslims. Each of these sects settled in various parts of what is now Lebanon. The Maronites and the Druze especially settled in the Lebanon Mountains where they have continued to vie for power up to the present day.

Between A.D. 1095 and 1291 some of the Christian countries of Europe, including England, France, Spain, and Belgium, launched six Crusades to recover Jerusalem and its surrounding areas from the Muslims. Allied with the Byzantine Army for the first Crusade in 1099, they attacked Antioch in Turkey and marched down the coast, capturing Tripoli,

ARABIC

Arabic is spoken today by about 200 million people, making it the world's fifth most popular language. By comparison, a billion speak Chinese; 460 million, English; 430 million, Hindi; and 300 million, Spanish.

The Semitic tribes of the Arabian Peninsula had been speaking Arabic for at least fifteen hundred years before they brought it north into what is now Lebanon. It is closely related to other languages that evolved in the same part of the world: Akkadian (Babylon and Assyria), Canaanite and Phoenician (Canaan/Phoenicia); Aramaic, the language of biblical times; Hebrew (Palestine); and Syriac (Syria).

By the time of the Islamic expansion, Arabic had evolved into two forms: the classic, written language based on Islamic scripture, and the spoken language used in everyday speech. It is still that way today. The Arabs consider their written language sacred and a symbol of Arab identity and unity. Although modern standard Arabic has been changed somewhat to make it easier to use and to include modern words, it is still the official language of religion, literature, public speeches, and radio and television. It is read from right to left.

Arabic is spoken, however, in many dialects (regional variations of a language, distinguished by vocabulary, grammar, and pronunciation). The Lebanese speak a dialect strongly influenced by Syriac, which was influenced by Aramaic. Within Lebanon, Arabic dialects differ from region to region, with the Druze having the most distinctive.

Both the Arabic and the Roman alphabets grew out of the early Phoenician alphabet. While the Greeks and the Romans added vowels, the Arab scholars did not. The Arab alphabet includes eighteen beautifully scripted letters, all consonants. Vowels are created by adding dots or dashes above or below the line, making twenty-eight letters in all. Sometimes the dots or dashes are left out and it is up to the reader to interpret the vowel based on the context of the word. For this reason, and because some sounds are unknown in other languages, Arabic can be difficult to spell consistently in other languages. In English, for example, the same Arabic word can be spelled in several different ways. Market can be suk, souk, suq, or souq. The city of Jounieh is also spelled Jounie or Junyah. The Koran is also spelled Quran, Quoran, or Qur'an.

Some Arabic words that have made their way into English include algebra, alcohol, alchemy, and zero, reflecting the early Arab progress in science, especially mathematics and astronomy. The word assassin comes from the Arabic *hashisin* (hashish-eaters), a sect of fanatics who killed crusaders.

Beirut, Sidon, and Tyre between 1109 and 1124. For the next two hundred years they ruled the coastal parts of Syria, building castles, churches, and towers. Using the local Maronite Christians as allies whom they brought into union with the

Catholic Church in Rome, the crusaders introduced Western ideas. This created more divisions between local Christians and Muslims, a foreshadowing of future wars between the two groups.

By the thirteenth century, both the crusaders in Europe and the Arab empire based in Baghdad had begun to lose power as they fought off Mongol tribes from Central Asia and the Mamluks from Egypt.

THE MAMLUKS

The Mamluks were a Central Asian people who had been captured by the sultans of Egypt to serve as bodyguards and warriors. In 1252 a Mamluk warrior named Muez-Aibak assassinated the Egyptian sultan and founded a new Mamluk dynasty. By 1260 he and his followers had moved north and taken over Syria. By the end of the thirteenth century, they had expelled the last of the crusaders from the coastal cities.

The castle of Sidon (pictured) is one of several castles the Crusaders built throughout Lebanon to help defend land wrested from the Muslims.

They divided the Syrian territory into six provinces called *mamlakas* which they oversaw for the next three hundred years. The Sunni Muslims' basic system of government was feudal, one in which local rulers and landowners (called lords in Europe and chiefs or sheikhs in the Middle East) protected people in exchange for taxes, respect, and loyalty. Unlike European feudalism, Islamic feudalism did not allow landowners to pass on their property to their children and thus develop into powerful aristocracies.

The Druze under the Mamluks were an exception to this, however. Their form of feudalism resembled the European type, which the Mamluks tolerated. According to Lebanese historian Kamal Salibi:

> The central government invested the leading Druze chief of his day with some formal authority, technically as an officer of the sultan's provincial cavalry. But this modest position was far exceeded by the local power and prestige which such a chief enjoyed. As supreme emir [local governor], the paramount Druze chief headed a feudal system based on hereditary land tenure, and was the overlord of a number of feudal families who controlled the various Druze districts.[5]

This allowed the Druze to become a powerful force in Lebanon up until the 1700s, even under Sunni Muslim rulers. For the most part they lived peacefully, separate from the other large communities of Maronites and Shiites. Occasionally the Mamluks tried to redistribute the population to prevent any one group from becoming too powerful. One ruler brought in more than three hundred nomadic tribes from Persia and settled them on the coast between Tripoli and Beirut. Another brought in Sunni Turks to watch over the Shiites. None of this changed the basic nature of Lebanon, however, where the different groups clung fiercely to their individual identities and territories.

During this era, the area of future Lebanon prospered intellectually and economically. Beirut became a major trading center between the Middle East and the European countries who wanted their raw materials and luxuries. By the sixteenth century, the area was attracting yet another major force in the north, the Turks.

The Ottoman Turks

The Ottoman Turks were also former slaves and warriors who fled from Turkistan in central Asia in the twelfth century when it was invaded by Mongol tribes. The name Ottoman means

The Father of Modern Lebanon

The Ottoman Turks ruled their empire, including Syria and Lebanon, with an iron grip. When they opened their hands, it was to accept tribute in the form of payment from their many governors, or emirs, who had been granted positions of power and who in turn expected payment from those below them.

Most of these emirs did as they were told, not wanting to lose their many advantages. One exception was Fakhr ad-Din al-Mann II (Fakhreddine) who tried to expand his territory both geographically and culturally.

Born in the Chouf Mountains in 1570, Fakhreddine was part of the powerful Mann family. Although born a Druze, he was raised by Maronite Christians after his father was killed. When he became an emir in 1590 (by offering money to the sultan), his territory included Beirut, Sidon, and the Chouf Mountains. Before long his governorship moved north to include the Qadisha Valley and Tripoli, and by 1605 it had expanded in all directions to include parts of Palestine, Jordan and Syria, Mount Lebanon, and the coastal cities.

A small man with a cautious nature, he nevertheless was called the Sultan of the Mountain by the Turkish sultan in Constantinople. He became very wealthy and built an army of forty thousand mercenary soldiers. He also had a large vision for Lebanon, modernizing the ports, increasing trade with Europe, and developing a silk industry.

In the early years of his rule, Fakhreddine was left alone by the Turkish rulers who were busy fighting with the Persians. In 1613 he was exiled for five years to Italy for entering into a secret agreement with the Duke of Tuscany who had promised his support for Lebanese autonomy. While living there he absorbed many Western ideas, including technical advances from Italian architects and engineers. After a more friendly governor took over in Damascus, Fakhreddine returned home. He continued promoting the advancements he had studied in Italy, including better buildings and bridges, improved irrigation, and farming methods. He upgraded the production of olive oil and encouraged the Maronites to move farther south to work in the silk industry. He welcomed new religious groups from Europe and tried to merge the wide variety of religious groups into one community. The economy flourished.

Now considered a nationalist hero—the father of modern Lebanon— Fakhreddine was not appreciated by the tight-fisted, closed-minded Turks. Eventually they sent the Syrian and the Egyptian governors to attack him. Fakhreddine fled to a cave in the mountains but was captured in 1633 and taken to Istanbul. Two years later, he was executed.

"house of Osman" from the founder of the Turkish Empire, Osman Khan Ghazi. They settled in Anatola (now Turkey) and conquered Constantinople (now Istanbul) in 1453, thus ending the Byzantine Empire. In 1516 they invaded Syria and established a semiautonomous state. Called Greater Syria, it included what is now Syria, Lebanon, Jordon, and Israel and was ruled by a provincial governor, or *pasha*.

The Ottomans oversaw Syria for the next four hundred years under two related families: the Manns and the Shihabs. The Manns were Druze Muslims who lived on the southwestern slopes of the Lebanon Mountains. Originally from Damascus, they had helped the Arabs defend the mountains against the crusaders in the twelfth century and been a part of the Mamluk army. The Ottomans allowed the Druze to practice the feudal system of government they had enjoyed under the Mamluks and they remained politically dominant throughout the state. The Maronites either imitated their system or settled nearby and went to work as peasants for the Druze. During the 1600s and 1700s the Druze sometimes fought among themselves, as families competed for positions of power.

In 1697, when the Manns were unable to produce an heir, power shifted to another part of the family—the Shihabs. The Shihabs were Sunni Muslims who settled in southern Lebanon. During the 1700s the Ottoman Empire began to weaken. Many rebellious emirs tried to expand their power from neighboring states such as Egypt and Palestine. The Druze continued to fight among themselves and some rebelled against the Shihab rulers.

ENTER THE EUROPEANS

During this time several European countries and Russia became interested in the Middle East. Since crusader times, the French had felt a special bond with the Maronites. Some even speculated that the Maronites were a lost tribe from France. Strong Catholics, the French declared themselves the protectors of the Christians in Lebanon in 1648 and a few years later appointed a Maronite sheikh as their representative in Beirut. This representation continued for more than one hundred years. When the ruling Shihab emirs converted to Maronite Christianity in 1770, the bond became stronger. In the late 1700s the French emperor

Napoléon invaded Egypt and attempted to invade Syria but was defeated. This increased tensions between the Druze and the Maronites. Already feeling their loss of power under the Shihab leaders, the Druze resented the Maronites' relationship with the French. The British lent their support to the Ottomans to defeat the French and began to ally themselves with the Druze. Even the Russians became involved. At war with Turkey, they encouraged rebellions in Palestine and Syria.

Since the end of the eighteenth century, foreign powers have played an integral part in Lebanon's history. According to historian Salibi:

> From 1770 onwards, there was scarcely an event in Syria or any other part of the Ottoman Empire which remained the purely internal concern of local chieftains and Ottoman officials. As the rivalry between the European Powers in the Near East developed, such local events acquired an international importance and attracted attention abroad. Russia, Britain, France and Austria intervened everywhere. But in the nineteenth century nowhere did conditions invite intervention more than in Lebanon where feudal quarrels and sectarian tension provided ample material for crisis.[6]

In many ways, the people of Lebanon benefited from European influences during the nineteenth century. Some, especially the Maronites, studied in Europe and returned to establish schools or become private tutors. British and American Protestant missionaries also established schools, including the first one for girls and a college that was to become the best in Lebanon: the American University of Beirut. Up until 1850 most of the people, including leaders, could not read. Books were still copied by hand. Finally, when the Arabic printing press was able to produce more books and more schools were established, the province of Syria/Lebanon became the most advanced in the Ottoman Empire. The majority of people learned to read and there was a revival of literature.

Politically, however, the nineteenth century brought turmoil, foreign meddling, violence, the end of the Shihab regime, and a transitional form of government that would take the area into the twentieth century. During the 1830s

Egypt invaded and occupied Syria, temporarily uniting the Maronites and Druze in their mutual dislike for the Egyptians. Turkey, Britain, and Austria sent in more than eight thousand five hundred troops to fight the Egyptians. After their common enemy withdrew, the Druze and the Maronites began to turn on each other. The Druze had suffered even more loss of power and property under the Egyptians and resented the Maronites who were having their own internal squabbles over leadership. Between 1840 and 1860 fighting broke out everywhere between the Maronites and Druze. Attempts by the Ottomans or by foreign leaders—from the French to the British to the Austrians—to introduce government reforms to balance power between the different groups failed miserably. Many times people did not even know why they were fighting. One packhorse accidentally bumping into another was enough to set off a village war. And, according to historian Salibi, each incident brought in more foreign intervention: "Our affairs have become the concern of Britain and France. If one man hits another the incident becomes an Anglo-French affair, and there might even be trouble between the two countries if a cup of coffee gets spilt on the ground."[7] Even the Russians got in on the act, trying to help the Greek Orthodox when the Sunnis and Shiites turned on them.

French warships land in Beirut in 1861 to restore order in the aftermath of Druze massacres of Christians.

SURPRISE ATTACKS

One American missionary, Henry Jessup, described the fear many Christians felt in 1860 when the Druze were attacking Christian villages. In this account, quoted by historian Kamal Salibi in *The Modern History of Lebanon*, the Druze had waited fifteen years to take revenge and kill one particular man. Although they destroyed property, burning down houses, they did not kill anyone else.

On Saturday the 26th, we made an American flag to hoist over the mission premises in case the hordes should invade this district.... The whole population were in a state of apprehension. Bodies of armed Druses, horse and foot, marched from village to village, singing their weird war song.... On Sunday, May 27th ... we went down to the little church under Mr. Calhoun's house.... It was my turn to preach. I looked down on a company of anxious faces. I had begun the service and was reading the first verse of "My Faith looks up to Thee" when the report of a gun nearby, followed by a scream, startled the congregation. Just then a man ran by the church door shouting, "Abu Shehadan is killed! Rise and run for your lives!'" That church was emptied in a moment. It has been agreed beforehand among the Protestants, Greeks and Maronites, that if any Christian was killed in Abeih they would all run en masse down the steep mountain descent of six miles to Moallakah, a large Maronite village on the seashore and thence twelve miles to Beirut. So no time was needed for consultation. The entire male Christian population fled, over walls, terraces, vineyards and through pine groves and the rocky slope, avoiding the roads.... Not a Christian man or boy over ten years was left in the village. As the Druses never touch women in their wars, the Christian women and girls all remained.

By the late 1850s the area of Lebanon was in complete turmoil, and the Druze began attacking Christians everywhere. Even though the Druze army was outnumbered fifty thousand to twelve thousand, they were better organized and used surprise tactics to overwhelm the Christians. In one four-week period, 11,000 Christians were killed, 4,000 died of starvation, and more than 100,000 were left homeless. Many Christians fled to Beirut, but even there they were taunted by the Muslims and many left the country. Off the coast appeared British, French, and other European warships.

After eight months of discussion in 1861 between France, Russia, Prussia, Austria, and the Ottomans, a reorganized form of government was established for the area of Mount Lebanon. This did not include Beirut, the Bekaa Valley, Tripoli in the north, or Sidon in the south. Led by a Christian Catholic *mutesarrif* (governor) appointed by the Ottomans, the government also included a council with twelve representatives from different sects, called the Mutesarrifate. This form of government carried the beginnings of present-day Lebanon into the twentieth century. It was modern and efficient and restored calm to Lebanon. Many social and economic reforms were introduced; new roads were built and agriculture and trade prospered. Many Lebanese who had emigrated to North or South America sent back or returned with money, which also helped the economy.

As the Mutesarrifate of Mount Lebanon grew and prospered, the area of Lebanon finally became more than just a name for a mountain range. Although it was still technically part of Syria, it was taking on a new identity as a distinct political unit. As described by historian Salibi, "Thus, at long last, Lebanon ceased to be a mere geographic expression and became the official and internationally recognized name of a territory of special administrative character within historical Syria."[8]

During this time the idea of Lebanon as a nation began to take hold, especially among the Christians. This idea was encouraged by French religious and political leaders. In addition, many began to resent that the *mutesarrif* was not Lebanese and that the territories of Beirut and the Bekaa Valley had been taken away. They wanted a new country with expanded frontiers.

As the twentieth century dawned, the Ottoman Empire was beginning its decline. Although they had lost their firm grip on the territory of Lebanon, they left a permanent imprint. Lebanon was, unlike any other Arab territory, a restless mix of Christians and Muslims, of village tribal groups, and sophisticated city dwellers. A link between old and new cultures and between those who had passed through from every direction, Lebanon was about to go in search of a new identity.

In Search of a Modern Identity

The Mutesarrifate of Mount Lebanon lasted sixty years from the time it was created in 1861 until the area was taken from the Ottomans after World War I. It was after this event that Lebanon began to acquire a distinct identity for the first time. This identity would be challenged in the twentieth century as Lebanon was repeatedly shaped by its own people from within and by competing countries from outside.

The Growth of Nationalism

Like Lebanon, many provinces within the Ottoman Empire wanted to break away and become self-governing nations. This idea, called nationalism, took hold in the early nineteenth century. Some Ottoman provinces like Greece and Serbia were able to become independent. Unlike Lebanon, they were close to European countries that offered military support, and they were more unified; the people all spoke the same language and followed the same religion. In Lebanon, half the people were Christians and half were Muslims. Although they had lived together peacefully for centuries, they had begun to fight for representation and positions of power as the Ottoman government tried to include all groups fairly. They also had different ideas about nationalism.

The Christians did not like the Ottomans or Islam and began to push for the creation of a separate Lebanese Christian nation. The Maronites in particular were encouraged by the French. Some Christians, especially the Greek Catholics and the Greek Orthodox, wanted to include Syria. Most wanted to expand the frontiers of Mount Lebanon to include Beirut, the Bekaa Valley, Tripoli in the north, and Sidon in the south.

The Muslims did not particularly like the Ottomans either, but they did enjoy their special status as fellow Muslims and so did not support the Christian nationalist movement. They began to promote an Arab nationalist movement instead. They saw Lebanon as part of a larger Muslim Arab empire. To them, being an Arab and being a Muslim were the same thing. Although many Christians began to support the Arab nationalist movement because they thought it would help them acquire more land, they were also suspicious because they also considered themselves Arabs and because they did not want to be dominated by Islam. So although the idea of nationalism began to grow in Lebanon, it was not a single, solid idea shared by all its people. In order to create a new identity, they would have to try to agree first on its definition. This would emerge after World War I.

WORLD WAR I

Turkish troops follow a standard bearer during World War I. Lebanon was brought into the conflict when the Ottomans sided with the Central Powers.

The area of Lebanon became involved in World War I when in 1914 the Ottoman Turks sided with Austria-Hungary, Germany, and Bulgaria (the Central Powers) against Russia, Britain, France, and the United States (the Allied Powers).

Although the war was fought mainly in Europe (the Western front) and Central Asia (the Eastern front), the Mutesarrifates of Lebanon and Syria suffered greatly. There the Ottomans suspended the representative form of government and replaced it with a harsh military occupation. In February 1915 the Turkish governor set up a blockade of the eastern Mediterranean to prevent supplies from reaching Allied forces. Thousands of Lebanese—one third of the country's population—died of starvation and plague. Tourism and business declined and the economy was devastated.

The war ended in the fall of 1918 when the British and Arab forces moved into Palestine and the Ottomans gave up their arms. Two years later the Allied powers met in San Remo, Italy, to divide up the conquered land, including the Ottoman Empire, and to form the League of Nations to oversee the results. The resulting plan, or mandate, gave control of Syria and Mount Lebanon to the French. Although the surrounding Arab countries objected because they wanted Arab countries to remain united, the idea was to prepare Syria and Lebanon for independence.

THE FRENCH MANDATE

During the war the French had maintained close contact with the Christian Lebanese nationalists, and now worked with them to define a new political state. On September 1, 1920, they announced the formation of the State of Greater Lebanon. As the nationalists had wanted, it was expanded to include the Bekaa Valley and the coastal cities of Beirut, Tripoli, Sidon, and Tyre. Based on an unwritten agreement called the National Pact, its government was an adaptation of the French parliamentary form, where representatives are elected to a council (like the American House of Representatives). Because there were so many religious sects in Lebanon, the representatives were to be picked according to their religion. In addition, the president was always to be a Christian. This system is called a sectarian (based on sects) or confessional (based on confessions) form of government. (Both "sects" and "confessions" refer to religious groups.)

This new identity for Lebanon pleased the Christians far more than the Muslims. The Christians were given more positions of power and more representatives, a six-to-five ratio.

Some Muslims outwardly protested and wanted to remain part of Syria. Eventually the Shiite Muslims realized they were better off as a large majority in Lebanon than they would be as a small minority in Syria. The Druze, however, staged several revolts, but because they were too small a group to be given positions of leadership, they retreated into the background and supported other Muslim protesters. To try to please everybody, the French governor and the elected representatives selected a Greek Orthodox to be the first president. Although both Christians and Muslims disliked the French control, Greater Lebanon was on its way to becoming a modern state. A constitution was drafted and a currency system set up.

In 1932 the Maronites insisted on conducting a census to prove they were in the majority. Although the census did back them up, the Muslims accused them of rigging the census for their own gain. For the next few years Greater Lebanon struggled through internal fighting. The constitution was suspended. Muslim groups increased their protests, some of which became violent. In reaction, some conservative Christians formed their own militia, called the Phalange. Muslims in turn organized a militia called the Muslim Scouts or Najjada. In an attempt to control violence, French and Lebanese leaders agreed in a new a treaty that Greater Lebanon should become independent by 1939. A new constitution was drafted and, for the first time, a Sunni Muslim was selected as Prime Minister. All this was put on hold, however, when Hitler's German forces invaded France in 1940 during World War II and set up a Nazi German–controlled government.

WORLD WAR II

For about a year, this German-controlled government also occupied France's mandated colonies, including Greater Lebanon. They were driven out in 1941 when the British and Free French (resistance fighters organized by General Charles de Gaulle) invaded Syria and Lebanon. Up until the end of the war in 1945, Greater Lebanon was used as a staging area for troops and supplies.

The Lebanese wasted no time in pressing for complete independence, however. With General de Gaulle's support, they declared themselves independent as soon as the Free French landed. Leaders met to draw up a new government under a new president. It did not acknowledge any French

General Charles de Gaulle inspects a unit of Free French troops. These resistance fighters helped to liberate Lebanon from Nazi control.

authority. In retaliation, the French arrested the new president and his cabinet and suspended the constitution. On November 22, 1943, under pressure from Britain, the United States, and various Arab states, the French relented and released the members of the new government. Lebanon was declared independent on January 1, 1944, although the official independence day is celebrated as November 22,1943. In 1945, after the war ended, Lebanon joined the United Nations and the League of Arab States. By the end of 1946 the French had withdrawn all administrative and military forces.

INDEPENDENCE

Lebanon was now known officially as the Lebanese Republic. For the next thirty years, the new country prospered. Although tensions continued between Christians and Muslims, attempts were made to balance power and to help the poorer Sunnis, Shiites, and Druze. More Muslims were appointed to important government positions. Women were given the right to vote in 1953. In the 1950s the country benefited from a liberal economic policy, a free exchange system, and a stable currency. Offering private bank accounts, Lebanon became the area's leading banking center, and was often called "the Switzerland of the Middle East," a reference to Switzerland's private banking system. In the southern city of Sidon, American oil companies financed and built the Trans Arabian Pipeline (TAPLINE) which carried oil more than a thousand miles from the Arabian Peninsula to tankers offshore and the Western countries beyond.

During the 1960s Beirut came to symbolize the free-spirited feeling of the times. Also called "the Paris of the Middle East" because of its beautiful Mediterranean coastline and climate, colorful nightclubs, and nearby mountain resorts, it attracted people from all over the Arab world and beyond. According to historian Kamal Salibi:

> Because of its free economic system, the wealth of the Arab Middle East converged there. . . . Its economy, which was mainly one of services, had an educated, trained and highly experienced infrastructure without parallel in any other Arab country; and Lebanese know-how everywhere became proverbial. Beirut, by the 1960s, had four universities, two of them of long standing, attracting Arab students from all directions. Its free press stood in a class of its own in the Arab world, and Lebanese newspapers and magazines were widely read from the shores of the Arabian Sea to those of the Atlantic. Lebanon, meanwhile, was making some notable progress in the industrial sector . . . . Beirut, by day and night, became the playground for rich Arabs.[9]

U.S. Marines monitor a Beirut neighborhood from a rooftop gun battery. Marines were sent to Lebanon in 1958 to stop violence between Christians and Muslims.

In spite of this success, however, problems continued to simmer under the glamorous surface of Lebanon. The Druze were feeling more alienated and powerless and formed the Progressive Socialist Party to represent them against the conservative Christians. Other Muslims began to demonstrate again in favor of Arab nationalism. Fighting finally broke out in 1958 between Christians and Muslims in Beirut and Tripoli, and the president appealed to the United States for help. About fifteen thousand marines were sent in to stop the violence.

By its third decade of independence, the new republic of Lebanon was beginning to show serious cracks in its facade. Pressured by forces from both inside and outside the country, it split apart in a devastating civil war that lasted from about 1975 to 1990.

THE PALESTINIAN-ISRAELI CONFLICT

One of the main causes of Lebanon's civil war was its misfortune to be caught in the middle of the conflict between the Palestinian refugees and the state of Israel. The Palestinian-Israeli conflict started in 1948 when the British withdrew from Palestine and the new country of Israel was formed for Jewish refugees. Up to 140,000 Palestinians, both Muslim and Christian, left, some by force, some by choice, moving north into Lebanon. At first the Lebanese welcomed these new settlers. Some, mostly Christians, were granted citizenship and allowed to work. The Maronites, however, soon began to resent the majority of the Muslim Palestinians, as they were upsetting the balance of power favored by the Christians. The Palestinians were moved into camps with basic housing, where many still live today. Their numbers increased in 1967 when Israel occupied the Palestinian territories in the West Bank (between Israel and Jordan) and again in 1970 when Jordan ordered all Palestinian guerilla fighters out of the country.

In 1964 the Palestinian Liberation Organization (PLO) was founded in Jerusalem by refugees and other Palestinians to represent the Palestinian people. The group has been led by Yasir Arafat since 1968, was recognized by the United Nations in 1974, and joined the League of Arab States in 1976. At first, their mission was to return Palestinians to their original homeland, now Israel. After the 1967 war in which Israel took over the West Bank, the PLO began to play a bigger role in Middle East politics. They wanted a land of their own and were willing to fight for it. They set up bases in Jordan and then in Lebanon, with headquarters in Beirut, becoming a state within a state. From Lebanon, they began launching attacks south into Israel. The Lebanese Armed Forces (LAF) did little to stop them because they were afraid of alienating the other Muslims in Lebanon.

THE LEBANESE ARMED FORCES

Like Lebanon itself, the Lebanese Armed Forces (LAF) had barely formed before collapsing in chaos. Originally part of the French military forces called the Legion of the Orient, the Lebanese developed into a sharpshooting unit. They remained a part of the French army until Lebanon took control as a new country in 1945. After independence, the LAF fought against Israeli invading forces in 1948 and managed to quell several internal uprisings for several more years.

Eventually, these uprisings became more severe as religious and political groups began to arm themselves. For the first few years of the civil war the LAF helped keep order, especially at the southern border with Israel. After Israel invaded Lebanon in 1982, the LAF began to weaken despite financial support and training from the United States. Its leadership was not strong enough to keep it from splintering into several camps. Many men formed their own militias or joined existing ones. In 1984 the LAF collapsed completely, a major blow to the government.

After the civil war most of the militias gave up their arms and disbanded. The LAF began to rebuild itself. President Emile Lahoud, a former military general, has made it a priority to rebuild and reorganize Lebanon's armed forces.

Currently, the LAF includes an army, navy, and air force with approximately 67,900 men. Unlike other parts of Lebanese life and government, it is not organized by religious sects.

Two Lebanese soldiers stand guard at a post near the Israeli border.

Israel began fighting back. They attacked refugee camps in the south and encouraged the Christian Phalange militia to attack two camps in Beirut, killing hundreds of refugees. When a Lebanese army officer defected, the Israelis recruited him and others, mostly Christians, to form the South Lebanese Army (SLA). They trained this group of about twenty-five hundred soldiers to occupy a six-mile security zone north of the border between Lebanon and Israel. In addition to protecting their own country, the Israelis saw themselves as the defenders of Lebanon's Christian majority. In 1982 they invaded Lebanon, enforcing what they called "Operation Peace in Galilee." Bombing Sidon and Tyre, they moved north into Beirut where they shelled and bombed the PLO headquarters in West Beirut for two months. British journalist Robert Fisk writes, "of all Beirut's sieges—by the Crusaders, by Saladin in the 12th Century, by the Anglo-Turkish fleet in 1840—none were on such a scale as the city's twentieth-century encirclement by the Israeli army."[10]

Yasir Arafat (left) visits PLO troops in Beirut. Throughout the 1970s, the PLO used Lebanon as a base from which to launch attacks against Israel.

They succeeded in driving out the PLO, who left with Arafat on ships for North Africa. In the meantime, several Christian and Muslim groups in Lebanon had taken up arms and begun to fight the Israelis and each other. For the next three years, until Israel withdrew most of its army in 1985, the country became a constant battleground. In Beirut, people were subjected to almost daily shelling from the surrounding Israeli army, warplanes overhead, and ships off the coast.

TAKING SIDES ALONG THE GREEN LINE

Even before Israel invaded, by the mid-1970s several religious groups had formed militias and were attacking each other. Some were incited by the Palestinian cause and some by old grudges. When the weak Lebanese army splintered apart these militias grew, attracting unemployed young men who were anxious to fight for a cause. Although there were more than forty of these militias by the end of the war, only a few played a significant role. For the most part, they were Christian versus Muslim. The Christian militias united as part of the Lebanese Front and included the Phalange, the Tigers, and the South Lebanese Army. Supported by Israel, they wanted the PLO out of Lebanon and did not want to share power in the country with any Muslims. The Muslim militias united as part of the Lebanese National Movement and included the PLO, the Progressive Socialist Party (a Druze organization), the Murabitoon (a Sunni group), and Amal and Hizbollah (radical Shiite groups). They supported the Palestinian cause as well as their own cause for more representation in the Lebanese government.

In 1975 the Christian and Muslim militias began attacking each other in Beirut. Unidentified gunmen killed four Christians in a church. In retaliation, the Phalange militia killed twenty-seven Palestinians on a bus. Soon the Phalanges were stopping all cars and slitting the throats of Muslims, including three hundred in one day that became known as Black Saturday. Fighting broke out everywhere on the streets, one militia pitched against another. In an attempt to control the violence, an Arab League peacekeeping force drew a Green Line (as used on military maps) down the middle of Beirut, creating a Christian section on the east side of the city and a Muslim section on the west. With armed checkpoints and barriers, this line divided the city until the

Rescue workers remove the body of a victim of a 1983 bombing of the American Embassy in Beirut. Lebanese Muslim extremists targeted Americans in retaliation for attacks by Christian militias.

end of the war and became an uninhabited zone of bombed-out buildings and overgrown weeds. People still crossed over from one side to another, but at great risk. Most of the Muslim militias set up their headquarters in the western half of the city and the Christian militias did the same in the east.

As fighting intensified in the south between Israel, the SLA, and the PLO, many Shiites moved north into the southern suburbs of Beirut. There they were attacked by Christian militias. In retaliation, their Amal and Hizbollah militias began kidnapping foreigners, mostly Americans. They also sent suicide bombers into the American Embassy, killing 63 and wounding 100, and into the marine headquarters, killing 265 American and 50 French forces. After the Israeli invasion in 1982, many Christian militias intensified fighting even in other parts of the country. In the Chouf Mountains, for example, they tried to take over from the Druze who had been there for centuries.

For the first few years of the civil war, battles were fought mainly along Christian-Muslim lines. Gradually, however, as attempts to form workable governments failed, complete anarchy took over. In 1988 one government formed in West Beirut and another in East Beirut. Christians began fighting other Christians and Muslims other Muslims within their own halves of the city. According to American journalist Thomas Friedman who was in Beirut at the time:

Syrian troops are welcomed into Beirut in 1976. Syria committed troops to both Christian and Muslim groups during Lebanon's civil war.

One could find Druze fighting Shiites for control of a particular West Beirut street on Monday, and Shiites fighting Sunnis for control of a neighboring street on Tuesday. Across the Green Line in East Beirut the same sort of confrontation was going on between the Christian Phalangist militia and the Christian-led Lebanese army as well as a host of smaller Christian factions.[11]

During this time, many thieves and gangsters also formed militias for criminal purposes. They took advantage of the lack of an army and police to do whatever they wanted, from stealing and smuggling goods to extorting and laundering money. In desperation, leaders turned to outside forces for help.

THE SYRIANS

Carved from the same historical and geographical area as Lebanon, Syria considered itself a protective "big brother" to Lebanon. When Christian leaders in Lebanon appealed for help in 1975, Syria sent in forty thousand troops. At first sympathetic with the Palestinians and their movement for a homeland, the Syrians changed their minds and turned on them instead, fearful of a war with Israel. In 1981 they changed sides again and helped the PLO attack the Phalange in the mountain city of Zahle. They also installed missiles in the Bekaa Valley, missiles that made the Israelis uncomfortable. Removing the missiles became one justification for their invasion in 1982. For the rest of the war, the Syrians withdrew to the background, fighting mainly in the Bekaa Valley and in the north near Tripoli. Since they were armed by the Russians, they also attracted fire from American warships (enemies with Russia in the Cold War during this time).

PEACEKEEPING FORCES

United Nations peacekeeping forces arrived in August 1982, after the Israeli invasion. The majority of them were American marines, accompanied by French and Italian soldiers. One of the leaders asking for their help was the PLO's Yasir Arafat. Knowing he was about to be evacuated from his headquarters in West Beirut, he wanted a safe escort. The soldiers watched over the Palestinians as they boarded ships, and then left Lebanon themselves. The peacekeepers were back a week later after the new Christian president—Phalange leader Bashir Gemayel—was killed by a bomb and Phalange militia entered two Palestinian camps and killed up to two thousand refugees. Although the multinational forces were at times provoked to take part in battles, including firing at Syrian and Muslim forces, their role remained mainly a peacekeeping one. When Bashir's brother Amin was selected as president—an unpopular choice with Muslims—the marines were seen as stooges of a government few liked. They left in February 1984 after the bombings of the American Embassy and the marines' headquarters.

CRUMBS OF NORMALCY

Daily life during the civil war for most people in Lebanon, especially those in Beirut, became a cross between a nightmare and a mind game. Hours or days of violence, during which people would stay inside, alternated with hours or days of peace. According to *New York Times* journalist Thomas Friedman, people learned to take advantage of these short breaks from the violence:

The minute a cease-fire took effect in one neighbor-hood, the storekeepers cranked up their steel shutters and life immediately mushroomed back onto the streets, as people grabbed for any crumb of normalcy they could—even if they knew it would last only an hour or a day. Beirutis always lived in this peculiar half-light between security and insecurity, war and truce in

THE LOST GENERATION

New York Times journalist Thomas Friedman won a Pulitzer Prize for his writing during the civil war in Lebanon. As described in *From Beirut to Jerusalem*, he often interviewed high school and college students. When he asked one group their names and ages, one replied, "We are all a hundred years old."

It must have seemed that way to the lost generation of Lebanese youth—those kids who were nine and ten when the civil war began. They were just really waking up to the world, starting to read newspapers, understand a little politics, and dream of what they wanted to be when the civil war de-scended in 1975 and destroyed their adolescence before they knew it was gone. One day they were kids, the next day they were adults. Chronologi-cal age meant nothing in Beirut. "Normal" for Lebanese youths meant studying for finals with the rock radio channel turned up louder than the shelling. "Normal" for them meant virtually never going out at night. "Normal" for them meant having at least three close friends and one rel-ative who had died a violent death. Few of them could distinguish be-tween Chuck Berry and Little Richard, or early Beatles and late Beatles, but by their fifteenth birthdays practically all of them could distinguish between a Katyusha rocket and a 155-mm mortar just by listening to the sound of the incoming whistle. While their parents knew a different life and would never really feel at home again without it, their kids had never known anything else and would never really feel whole again. . . .

This lost generation of Lebanese youth not only missed out on their adolescence; they also missed out on having a country. For them, most of Lebanon was a foreign country—just a picture on an old calendar in the attic or a faded postcard in the drawer—nothing they ever experi-enced, smelled, or touched. . . .

"My younger brother," said Tannir [a student who worked as a Red Cross volunteer, "is always asking me what is behind the Green Line. . . . He doesn't know. He doesn't know our house in the mountains. He has never climbed a tree in his life."

which there were always enough periods of quiet to go about one's day but never enough to feel confident that it wouldn't be one's last.[12]

Many learned to cope with a combination of humor, resignation, and reliance on family. Families and neighbors combined living quarters. Some displaced families moved into abandoned buildings or makeshift shantytowns. Many left Lebanon for other countries, inviting neighbors to move into their apartments or houses (those left empty would be broken into and occupied). Water and electrical services were often interrupted and people used generators or lined up at wells with pails to get water. The Lebanese became one of the world's highest users of Valium, sold over the counter like aspirin, without a prescription. Before venturing out anywhere in their cars, they listened to radio or television "road reports" (reports of bombings and fighting) just as in normal times they would listen to traffic reports. Those with money who needed things—from gourmet food to gasoline to passports—hired people called "fixers" who bribed their way though the maze of militias. Some people in rural areas suffered even more severely. Whole villages were left without running water, sewer systems, or electricity. Some were abandoned altogether as people moved into the cities. As the war began to wind down in the late 1980s, many Lebanese wondered if they would ever feel normal and live regular lives again.

WINDING DOWN: THE LAST YEARS OF THE WAR

By 1985 Israel began to withdraw its troops, leaving most of the fighting to Christian militias they had supported and to the SLA in the southern buffer zone north of the border. These militias continued fighting with the Druze and the Shiites near Sidon. In West Beirut, several of the Muslim militias fought with each other and with Palestinian soldiers who were returning to the city. The Shiite Amal militias especially did not want the Palestinians to return and provoke Israel's retaliation, and therefore attacked the refugee camps, killing thousands. By that time, the only powerful force left in Lebanon was Syria. True to their role of big brother, the Syrians moved back into West Beirut to negotiate a cease-fire and establish order. They managed to stop the Shiite attacks on the camps (although Amal continued to attack camps in the south up until 1988). In the meantime, outgoing president Amin Gemayel decided to appoint General Michel Aoun to lead a temporary military government. Aoun, who did not like the Syrians, tried to drive them out. In protest, several Muslim leaders, including a former prime minister, decided to form a rival government in West Beirut.

To many Lebanese, it now seemed as if the division of their country into separate Muslim and Christians sections was complete. During 1989 violence erupted again across Beirut's Green Line. Attempts by France to supply humanitarian aid and by Iraq to supply arms further complicated the situation. Finally, in the fall of 1989, three neighboring Arab countries—Algeria, Morocco, and Saudi Arabia—helped the Lebanese reach a peace settlement. Called the Taif Accord because the meeting was held in Taif, Saudi Arabia, the agreement called for an immediate cease-fire and for government reforms. Two

THE TAIF ACCORD

On October 22, 1989, the Lebanese National Assembly met with three Arab leaders—King Hassan of Morocco, King Fahd of Saudi Arabia, and President Chadli of Algeria—in Taif, Saudi Arabia, to propose a cease-fire and peace plan for the civil war in Lebanon. The resulting agreement became known as the Charter of National Reconciliation, or the Taif Accord. Although the accord was criticized by the current Lebanese military leader and by Druze and Shiite militias, it was accepted by the majority of Maronite and Sunni leaders and ratified on November 5. Divided into four parts, the plan's proposals helped end the war.

The first part of the plan restructured Lebanon's government to balance power more fairly between Christians and Muslims. Since Muslims were now in the majority in Lebanon, they would now share half the Cabinet posts and half of the seats in the National Assembly. In addition, the Christian president would share more power with the Sunni Muslim prime minister.

The second part of the plan listed the steps necessary for establishing government authority throughout Lebanon. These included disbanding the militias, rebuilding the internal security and armed forces, helping the Lebanese displaced by the war, and eventually withdrawing Syrian troops. Part three of the plan specified that Israel withdraw all occupying troops from Lebanon and that United Nations troops be stationed at the border to insure the safety of the area. The last, fourth part of the plan recognized the special relationship between Lebanon and Syria "based on the roots of close affinity, history and common interests." This special relationship meant that each country promised to uphold the security, independence, and unity of the other.

years later, the Lebanese also signed a Treaty of Brotherhood, cooperation and coordination with Syria allowing Syria to maintain troops in Lebanon. Since the end of the war, many of the Syrian troops have left, but not enough for most Lebanese who regard them as interfering big brothers.

REUNITED AT LAST

After signing the peace agreements, the Lebanese worked with the Syrians to restore authority over the country. They ousted General Aoun who protested the peace agreements and who continued fighting with Christian militias. In 1991 they removed the barriers on either side of the Green Line. The militias were forced to give up their arms and disband. Many soldiers rejoined the Lebanese Army, united for the first time in years. The following year all hostages were released and the Lebanese held elections for the first time in twenty years. Since then, peace has returned to most of Lebanon except the very south where periodic battles have erupted between the Muslim Hizbollah militia and Israeli troops. In May 2000, Israel finally withdrew its troops completely and the SLA collapsed, many fleeing into Israel.

General Michel Aoun led a short-lived military government toward the end of the civil war.

As a result of the civil war, between 125,000 and 150,000 Lebanese died, 75,000 were permanently disabled, and up to 1.5 million lost their homes. More than 17,000 disappeared and another 500,000 left the country. An additional 80,000 Palestinians entered the camps where there are now about 350,000 refugees.

Left with the wreckage of a country, the Lebanese have begun the process of rebuilding. It will not be easy as they examine the causes of the civil war and work to prevent another one. In addition, they are still being affected by outside forces as they move from being a link between empires to a country with its own strong, modern identity.

5

THE SHIFTING PATTERNS OF DAILY LIFE

If the people of Lebanon are like parts of a mosaic, their daily lives can be compared to a kaleidoscope. The many colorful parts do stand out from one another, but they keep shifting into an endless variety of patterns. Those who visit Lebanon with one set picture in mind most likely will be surprised. It is not completely traditional, as are many Arab countries, and it is not completely modern. It is an ever changing combination of old and new, a combination reflected in every aspect of Lebanese life, from government to dress.

GOVERNMENT IN LEBANON

Like the French model upon which is it based, the Lebanese government is a republic with a parliamentary form of government. It is also a sectarian form of government, structured so that several different religious sects are fairly represented.

The main legislative body is the one-house Parliament, or National Assembly, consisting of 128 members. Members are elected every four years. By constitutional law, half the assembly members are Christians and half are Muslims. As of 2002, the Parliament is comprised of: 34 Maronites, 27 Sunnis, 27 Shiites, 14 Greek Orthodox, 8 Greek Catholic, 8 Druze, 5 Armenian Orthodox, 2 Alewites, 1 Armenian Catholic, 1 Protestant, and 1 Christian Minority. Within the assembly there are no secret votes; all voting is done by a show of hands or by standing up and then sitting down.

The assembly members elect the president, who is the head of state. To be elected, the president must have at least two-thirds of the assembly's vote and be a Maronite Christian. The president serves a six-year term and cannot serve two terms in a row.

The president, in turn, appoints a prime minister as head of the government, with the approval of the National Assembly. The prime minister must be a Sunni Muslim and also serves a six-year term.

The president presides over a cabinet of about thirty ministers. With the prime minister and the speaker of Parliament, who must be a Shiite Muslim, the president shares power three ways for executive decisions.

The judicial system consists of four courts to handle civil, commercial, and criminal cases; a constitutional council to uphold the constitutionality of laws; and a Supreme Court to handle any charges against the president or prime minister. Juries are not used. Certain civil matters, such as marriages, divorces, and inheritance, are handled by separate religious courts.

Lebanon's current president is Emile Lahoud, elected in 1998. The country's eleventh president and an army general, he was the commander of Lebanon's armed forces. His father was the founder of the Lebanese army and a member of Parliament.

The current prime minister is Rafiq Hariri, a wealthy businessman who oversaw Beirut's reconstruction after the civil war.

Since there is no separation of church and state in Lebanon, everyone is identified by his or her religion. Identification cards specify one as either Christian or Muslim; the choice of no religion is not allowed.

LIFE IN THE CITIES

About 80 percent of the Lebanese live in cities, making Lebanon the most urbanized of the Arab countries. In general they lead more modern lives than those outside the cities. Even though they maintain close ties with their villages, they gradually let go of the traditional values which tie people more tightly together in the rural areas.

Lebanese President Emile Lahoud participates in a 2002 Arab Summit in Beirut.

Lebanon's largest city, Beirut, is coming to life again since the end of the civil war, intent on recapturing its once glamorous image. The Lebanese are famous for their love of life and they are not wasting any time. Now that there is no Green Line dividing the city, people come and go freely. In some areas, such as the Hama District around the University of Beirut, or along the oceanfront walkway, the Corniche, an assortment of people sit at cafés or stroll, jog, or Rollerblade. According to Insight Guides' *Syria and Lebanon:*

> There is one place where all Beirutis meet at all hours of the day and night—the Corniche, which has long been a place to escape the city and catch some fresh sea air. From 4 AM it is packed with joggers; by lunchtime, it is populated with office workers; in early afternoon the joggers return; and at sunset, couples and families come out for an evening stroll. As well as vendors of coffee, corn on the cob, fruit and sandwiches, the Corniche is where most of the city's famous beach clubs and expensive hotels can be found.[13]

For most of the 1.1 million Beirutis, however, life is not glamorous, and despite an outward exuberance, the scars of war remain. Most are trying to get on with their daily lives in a city where bombed-out buildings still stand next to new high-rises, where there are few repaired sidewalks but far too many cars polluting the air and crowding the streets. According to Richard Covington's article on Beirut in *Smithsonian* magazine, "With one car per every three residents, Lebanon has among the highest automobile densities in the world; 60 percent of the vehicles are in Greater Beirut. Inspection is unheard of, and noxious exhaust fumes periodically cast a gray-brown pall over the skyline."[14]

Although many are back at work (especially in banking, finance, advertising, manufacturing businesses, and tourism) they are finding their money does not go far. Housing, if it is available at all, is expensive. The cost of living is high. Beaches that were once available to everybody have been walled in by expensive resorts, a symbol to many of the growing divide between the rich and the poor, no longer buffered by a solid middle class. This middle class has eroded as many have left the country or are now struggling financially.

Besides these high-rise resorts, the wealthiest part of the city is still in the eastern section, where some of the French-named streets are lined with expensive shops and beautiful old sandstone houses with red tiled roofs. Unfortunately, many of these old houses are being torn down and replaced by modern apartment buildings.

The southern and eastern suburbs are also building up and spreading out, taking over land once used for growing crops. This sprawl has also caused a huge increase in the rodent population as their predators (small wild animals) are driven away. The suburbs are dominated by the Shiites, many of whom have moved up from the south. Since children age eight and over are allowed to work in Lebanon, many of the poorer families send their children to work. The boys work in manual jobs and the girls as maids. Some children in the worst slum areas peddle items on the street.

Many residents of Beirut live in bombed-out apartment buildings like this one long after the conclusion of the civil war.

The other large cities in Lebanon—Tripoli in the north and Sidon in the south—face many of the same problems as Beirut. They too are recovering from the civil war, rebuilding their businesses, including the old souks (marketplaces) to appeal to tourists. Both cities are dominated by Sunni Muslims and are more traditional than Beirut.

Two other smaller cities are Sur in the south and Zahle in the Bekaa Valley. Sur (originally called Tyre) is Lebanon's southernmost city, just a few miles north of the Israeli border. It was at one time the most important city in ancient Phoenicia.

SMOKING: LEGAL AND ILLEGAL

A common sight in Lebanese cafés and restaurants is a group of people sitting around a pipe, smoking. Called nargilehs, or hubble-bubble pipes, they usually contain a mild apple- or other fruit-flavored tobacco. Some smokers prefer darker, stronger tobacco. It is burned in the top part of the pipe with charcoal and the smoke cooled by water in the bottom part before being pulled in by the mouth. The name hubble-bubble comes from the bubbling sound the pipe makes while being smoked.

Although the pipes are often offered to guests, they are usually not shared. It is considered rude to light a cigarette from the burning coals.

During the civil war, more than a few Lebanese added the drug hashish to their tobacco. Cultivated in great quantity—up to ten thousand tons a year— these illegal crops made many farmers and families in the Bekaa Valley rich. They built big, fancy houses, even palaces. At first the Syrians helped protect these crops, but after the civil war the Syrians and the Lebanese government put an end to the industry. Farmers were forced to grow regular tobacco in-

stead, along with tomatoes, potatoes, and grains. Their incomes fell and many of the grand houses they built now stand empty.

Two Lebanese men play backgammon and smoke nargilehs in a Beirut café.

Originally Tyre was an island with defensive walls built around it. The city gradually became attached to land by the Middle Ages as the waters surrounding it filled with silt flowing down from the mountains. Since the formation of Israel in 1948 and the closing of the border, Sur has not done as well economically as Beirut and Sidon. It was badly damaged during the civil war and is now surrounded by many squatter settlements, as described by Siona Jenkins and Ann Jousiffe in *Lebanon*, a Lonely Planet guide: "Today, Tyre has

FROM *MAZZA* TO *BOOZA*: LEBANESE CUISINE

Although the Lebanese have succumbed to Western fast food (the Hard Rock Café is a favorite), their own cuisine enjoys a delicious reputation worldwide. It is a unique combination of fresh Middle Eastern foods and spices with French flavors thrown in for good measure.

Most Lebanese meals start with *mazza*, a selection of hot and cold appetizers which can be enough for a whole meal. Typical cold appetizers are: *tabboule*, a salad of cracked wheat, onions, tomatoes and parsley; *loubieh*, a French bean salad; *warak ainab*, grape leaves stuffed with rice and meat; and pickled vegetables and cheeses. Typical hot appetizers are *falafil*, balls of spiced and fried chickpeas; *fatayer*, triangular pastries stuffed with minced lamb; or *makanek*, lamb sausages. Various flat breads and dips usually accompany each meal. The breads are served plain or seasoned with spices and olive oil. They are often used to scoop food. Dips include *tahina*, ground sesame seeds; *hummus*, ground chickpeas seasoned with garlic and olive oil; or *labneh*, a thick yogurt with garlic and olive oil.

For their main courses, Lebanese meals usually include chicken, lamb, or fish and rice. Two popular dishes are *kebbah*, minced lamb and wheat formed into balls and baked or fried, and *shwarma*, spit-roasted and sliced lamb or chicken. Other include *sayadich*, fish on rice with onion and tahini sauce; *lahm meshwi*, grilled lamb kabobs; and *shish tawouq*, chicken on skewers.

Desserts include a variety of puddings, custards, and pastries, many filled or flavored with honey, spices, and nuts such as almonds, pistachios, walnuts, or pine nuts. These include *baklava*, diamond-shaped layers of pastry soaked in syrup and filled with crushed nuts, and *zinoud is-sitt*, a fat white pastry stuffed with cream. Many pastries are regional specialties, such as *sanioura*, a light, oval-shaped biscuit made in Sidon.

Popular Lebanese drinks include coffee, fruit juices, and '*araq*. Coffee is strong and served in small cups, Turkish style. Because so many citrus fruits are grown in Lebanon, their juices are widely enjoyed, especially orange juice. Others are *jellab*, made from raisins, and *ay ram*, a salty yogurt drink. The national alcoholic drink is '*araq*. Similar to the Greek ouzo or French Pernod, it is flavored with aniseed and served with water and ice.

The Lebanese buy many of these foods as snacks from street vendors, especially kabobs and *shwarma* wrapped in flat bread, and their own version of pizza, topped with meat, cheese, or sesame seeds and the famous Middle Eastern spices.

And to cool their palates, they can pick up homemade ice cream dipped in pistachio nuts served throughout the country in *booza*, ice cream parlors.

a picturesque harbor adjoining a lively souq and is the administrative center for a number of villages and towns, but much of the central area is surrounded by unplanned squatter settlements and the feeling of prosperity found in many other postwar Lebanese cities is absent."[15]

Zahle is Lebanon's largest inland city. It is located about fifty miles east of Beirut on the slopes of the Lebanon Mountains in the Bekaa Valley. It is a popular resort area, enjoyed for its mountain streams, flowers, vineyards, and riverside cafés. The majority of its eighty thousand residents are Greek Catholics.

LIFE IN THE RURAL AREAS

Life in most of the rural areas of Lebanon is more difficult than in the cities. The people are poorer. Many lost their homes or farms during the civil war when whole villages were destroyed or abandoned. The war also destroyed their basic services such as garbage and sewage. As a result, much of the water—when there is running water—is contaminated. This has led to an increase in diseases such as hepatitis, dysentery, and even typhoid. Southern Lebanon is dotted with many makeshift communities: Palestinian refugee camps and settlements and other temporary squatter settlements of people displaced by the war. In the northern part of the country, many people work for the army, which has several military installations in the area. Many villages lack electricity. There is no tourism and the economic outlook is bleak.

FARMING IN LEBANON

For centuries, farming was the backbone—up to 40 percent—of Lebanon's economy. With its "breadbasket," the Bekaa Valley, and its fertile coastal plain, Lebanon's farmers prospered. Now, as a result of the civil war and soil erosion, farmers make up only about 7 percent of Lebanon's workforce. During the civil war some of the most lucrative crops were opium poppies and marijuana, which the government and the Syrians outlawed in the early 1990s. Many of the small and isolated villages are still without sewer systems. This and the overuse of pesticides have caused widespread contamination and a high rate of intestinal disorders.

Soil erosion has also eroded the quality of life where villages farm on terraced slopes. Nearly half of Lebanon's agriculture

Lebanese farmers harvest marijuana during the civil war. The drug was grown in great quantities until it was outlawed in the early 1990s.

is cultivated this way, and up to 25 percent of it has been lost. Although attempts at replanting forested areas will help prevent soil erosion, it is a slow process.

Many farmers moved to Beirut during the civil war and are slowly returning to their land. Some continue to work in the cities while they rebuild their farms. According to Marilyn Raschka, a journalist who interviewed such a farmer,

> One could argue that returning to farming should be a fairly simple move; after all, the land is still there. Those who rushed back to their properties after the fighting ended in 1990, however, were sadly disappointed. Villages were totaled, terraces and groves and fields were mined, water lines had been wiped out intentionally or through shelling. For my ticket collector [referring to his job in Beirut at a movie theater] / farmer friend, neglect over more than a decade meant that his olive and fruit trees were half-dead. No irrigation and no pruning had taken their toll.[16]

Despite these drawbacks, farming families, mostly Shiite Muslims, are producing crops of potatoes, tomatoes, citrus fruits, walnuts, tobacco, and grapes. Several are turning their grapes into wine and winemaking has become a profitable business in the Bekaa Valley. In the south, along the coastal plain, Shiite farmers grow citrus fruits, olives, and bananas. As part of its rebuilding efforts, the government is allotting funds to help these farmers get started again and to practice safer forms of farming without harmful pesticides.

LIFE IN THE CAMPS

By far the poorest and the most downtrodden of the people in Lebanon are the Palestinian refugees who live in camps and settlements throughout the country. Currently there are approximately 350,000 Palestinians in Lebanon. About half of these refugees live outside the camps and half within. Some of those living outside the camps have been able to find housing (especially if they have money), but many live in settlements near the camps. Refugees both inside and outside the camps receive economic and administrative aid from the United Nations Relief and Works Agency (UNRWA).

Palestinian children play in a Lebanese refugee camp. Refugees in Lebanon have no civil rights and limited opportunities for work.

THE CHICLETS CHILDREN: BEGGING FOR EDUCATION

Outside the shantytown near the Beirut refugee camps, many children sell Chiclets gum. Some have been put to work by their parents and some are begging for money to attend school. One American doctor, Agnes Sanders, has been trying to help these *nawar*, or gypsy children, by building and running a school for them. She was interviewed in the Beirut *Daily Star*:

What to do about the beggar children? Does buying their Chiclets encourage them to work or to beg? Either way, it's not easy to ignore them, though the government seems to have done just that. . . .

Who are these children and where do they come from? Sanders has compiled statistics on 50 of the around 200 families in the shantytown. . . . From these 50 families, only two or three fathers work at any given time. Mothers average nine children. And despite what's commonly thought, most children have at least one Lebanese parent. Still, they lack the official status needed for public education.

One reason for this is that to be officially recognized, a marriage between Muslims must be registered before both sheikh and the civil authorities. For children born to a second wife, whose only proof of marriage is often a promissory note signed by the man, chances are slim of ever becoming legal.

"People don't realize that these are children who have never done a puzzle, and don't know what it means to wait in [line]", Sanders says. "We believe these kids' parents will come to understand that having one educated child who can care for himself and for them in their old age beats having 10 uneducated, unemployable children. . . . The challenge for us has been keeping the kids here. . . . In September, the parents beg us to take them. But a few weeks later, we see the kids on the street begging or playing football."

The families have varied beliefs about putting children to work. While some of the most destitute would never send their children out to beg, begging for others is a family profession.

Today there are twelve camps throughout Lebanon: two north of Tripoli, one near Baalbak, four in and around Beirut, two near Sidon, and three near Sur.

The refugees inside these camps lead extremely difficult lives. Unwanted by the Lebanese, they have no citizenship, limited work and education, and poor health care. According to a report by the World Health Organization, they have the worst dental health in the world. A large percentage of the young men are paraplegics or amputees wounded in the war, but there are very few wheelchairs, crutches, or prosthetic limbs available to help them.

EDUCATION

With one of the highest literacy rates in the Arab world (more than 86 percent) and a young population (50 percent under the age of twenty-five), Lebanon has made education a high priority. There are twenty-one universities, including the multicultural and highly respected American University of Beirut established by American missionaries in the nineteenth century.

All Lebanese children are required to attend the first five years of primary school and up to 90 percent remain in school until the age of fourteen. After that, children can choose between academic schools (similar to American high schools) or vocational schools, and the enrollment rate drops to about 60 percent when many go to work, especially in family businesses. Because free public schools have a poor reputation, more than half of all Lebanese children attend private schools. In Beirut, the rate is even higher because only 11 percent of the schools are public. This is a problem for poor families who cannot afford to send their children to the better schools.

FAMILY LIFE

The Lebanese place great importance on family life, even more so since the civil war forced many to spend more time together in close quarters. If they are fortunate enough to have money, they are expected to help their poor relatives. They usually hire family members to work in their businesses. The family is considered a source of honor and status and consequently marriages are often arranged for practical rather than romantic reasons, to further the standing of the family. Young people are not encouraged to be independent and are expected to live at home until they marry, which for women is usually in their early twenties and for men, up to their late thirties. In rural areas, people marry earlier, and many marry first cousins (on their father's side) from the same village. Since marriage, divorce, and inheritance laws

are handled by the separate religious courts, there is no such thing as a marriage outside a church in Lebanon. For this reason, up to 22 percent of couples elope to Cyprus, where they can get married without a religious ceremony.

Children play by a river while their parents smoke nargilehs. The Lebanese family is a very close-knit unit.

For the most part, families are patriarchal. The father is considered the head of the household and is often very strict. Muslim men are allowed to have more than one wife but very few (about 3 percent) do because it is no longer financially feasible or socially acceptable. Lebanese Christian women live and dress in a more modern fashion than their Muslim counterparts, and many more work. In rural areas, even though many women work side by side with their husbands, they still are defined as wives and mothers.

THE ROLE OF WOMEN

The role of women in Lebanese society—both Christian and Muslim—is still defined primarily by family relationships: sister, daughter, wife, and mother. During the civil war, women began to play a stronger economic role as they went to work to help support their families. Since then, the number of women in professions has doubled. According to one United Nations report, women in Lebanon make up 51 percent of the country's pharmacists, 24 percent of lawyers, 15 percent of doctors, 14 percent of dentists, and 6 percent of engineers. Overall, however, they only make up 15 percent of the country's workforce. Very few hold positions of power in government or business. Only three of the 128 members of Parliament are women. There are two female ambassadors but no female cabinet ministers. Lebanese women gained the right to vote in 1953. According to historian William Harris in *Faces of Lebanon:*

> Only one woman—the Druze matriarch of the 1920s, Nazira Jumblatt—has registered as a prominent individual in Lebanon's story. For both Christians and Muslims, it has been a story of absolute and unrelenting male domination of the public arena. Even the war years and their shabby aftermath have not provided any significant assessment of women's perspectives and protest. Women received the vote in 1953, but there has not yet been any sign that they can make a relevant political impact.[17]

The Druze matriarch led her community for a short time only. She inherited the position when her husband was killed and relinquished it again when her son was old enough to take over.

In recent years the Lebanese constitution has been amended to eliminate all forms of discrimination against women, and many civil groups in Lebanon are focused on women's issues. Compared to most Arab countries, where women are severely restricted, Lebanese women are freer and have more opportunities.

Culturally, however, they still have some catching up to do. Sons are preferred in most families and are granted more privileges than daughters. A Muslim man can divorce his wife for not bearing sons. Lebanese women still cannot pass on citizenship to their children; it must come from their fathers. There are few places for Lebanese women to turn if they suffer domestic abuse. In fact, up to eighty Lebanese women a year are murdered by male relatives who feel justified in punishing their sisters, wives, or daughters for any suspicious activity they feel has brought shame to the family. Suspicious activity can be defined as anything from having coffee with a man in a café, to eloping with someone their family does not like, to committing adultery. Until recently, the Lebanese Penal Code allowed these "honor crimes" to go unpunished. The code has been amended but still includes enough loopholes that men can get away with lighter punishments. The Penal Code still specifies a longer prison sentence for a woman caught committing adultery (from three months to two years) than for a man (one month to one year). In addition, more proof is required to arrest a man for adultery than a woman.

DRESS

One of the best ways to see the shifting patterns of Lebanon's people is to watch what they are wearing. Traditional and modern walk side by side, especially in Beirut. According to Richard Covington's article on Beirut in *Smithsonian* magazine, "A pair of young women walk on the street: one covered head to toe in black hejab, chatting on her cell phone, the other, in a miniskirt, concentrating on avoiding the traffic."[18] Usually it is the Christian women who are dressed much as they would be in any Westernized part of the world. The Muslim women, on the other hand, dress more conservatively, ranging from a full cloak or long dress and veil to a modern dress with a head scarf. Their dresses are usually long and they often wear sandals or other modern footwear. Men, whether Christian or Muslim, usually wear more modern clothing, from blue jeans and T-shirts among the young to slacks and shirts and business suits for older men. Some Muslim men wear a head covering called the *kaffiyeh*, a head scarf that usually falls over one shoulder.

The older men and women in the Druze community still wear traditional costumes. The men wear high, round hats called *tarboosh*, long striped overcoats called *aba*, baggy pants that are fitted below the knee called *sherwal*. The women wear long dresses and drape their heads with sheer white veils.

In the rural agricultural areas, Western dress has become commonplace, with many people now wearing jeans, work boots, and gloves. Traditionally, Lebanese peasant women

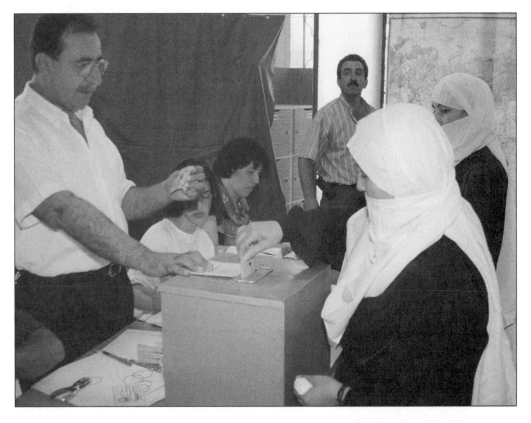

A veiled Druze woman casts her vote in a parliamentary election. Older members of the Druze community continue to wear traditional dress.

wore long fitted pantaloons with ruffles at the ankle; over these they wore a long-sleeved, knee-length dress and apron. All of these were in brightly colored calico prints. They tied black veils to their heads with a folded scarf. Today these women still wear calico scarves, usually under straw hats.

This nod to tradition, updated with the modern and practical, is another example of Lebanon's ever changing and vibrant people. As one Lebanese wrote, returning for a visit after twenty-five years,

> Whatever your view and whatever the measure of hope and anticipation, one thing is certain. Life in Lebanon is . . . more intense than anywhere else. The days last longer, are more colorful, surely more noisy—but somehow more happy—than any other place I know.[19]

CELEBRATING LIFE WITH ARTS AND ENTERTAINMENT

6

In spite of the many challenges facing the Lebanese in the coming years—from living daily life to rebuilding their country—they know how to celebrate life in a variety of ways. As with much else in Lebanon, this variety reflects the country's colorful mixture of cultures and attitudes. Depending on their tastes or moods, the Lebanese can and do enjoy anything from a village folk dance to a major league soccer game to an experimental play or art exhibit in Beirut.

SPORTS

The Lebanese are enthusiastic sports fans and especially love football (what Americans call soccer) and basketball. They have been playing and watching soccer games since 1910, when students from the American University beat players from a British ship anchored offshore. Since 1933, when local football teams formed a national federation, just about every village, town, or city has been represented by one or more teams. The best players are recruited for one of the two major teams—the Beirut Nejmeh or the Beirut Ansar—who play at the Sports City Complex. According to travel writers Siona Jenkins and Ann Jousiffe, "Beirut traffic is noticeably lighter when a team from the local league is playing."[20] In 2000, Lebanon hosted the Asian Cup finals.

Basketball games are also well attended and there are three major basketball teams: La Sagesse, Rosary, and Antranic. Another popular sporting event is horseracing, which draws crowds on Sundays to the Hippodrome in Beirut, one of the only places in the Middle East for placing a bet.

The Lebanese love cars and driving, especially *fast* driving. According to travel writers Siona Jenkins and Ann Jousiffe:

Lebanese soccer players celebrate a victory. Soccer is one of the most popular sports in the country.

The first rule of driving in Lebanon is: forget rules. Driving is on the right side of the road, unless the vehicles in front are not fast enough, in which case one drives on the left. The horn is used liberally because nobody uses their mirrors. There is no speed limit and moving violations do not exist. In other words, anarchy is the name of the game.[21]

Two car rallies a year are held in Lebanon: the Rallye du Printemps (Spring Rally) in Kesrouane (a mountainous area northeast of Beirut) and the Rallye des Cedres (Cedars Rally), in the Qadisha Valley. Plans are underway to host the first Middle East Formula One Grand Prix in 2003. It would race through the streets of Beirut, finishing in the renovated downtown area.

The Lebanese also love water sports: waterskiing, windsurfing, sailing, and swimming in the Mediterranean, and rafting and kayaking in the rivers. Unfortunately there are few public beaches left, and only one in Beirut. Most have been taken over by private hotels and resorts where only those with money can swim off their concrete jetties or enjoy their private swimming pools. One public swimming area is accessible through an underground tunnel from the University of Beirut.

From November to May, many Lebanese enjoy skiing at the six ski resorts located in the mountains, one in the north part of the country and five close to Beirut. Many Beirutis who ski, drive there and back in one day.

From May to October the mountain areas offer many other sporting opportunities for the adventurous: paragliding, hiking, mountain biking, and spelunking (exploring caves). At least four hundred caves have been discovered in Lebanon so far, some of deepest in the Middle East.

Hunting is a popular pastime and has taken its toll on the wildlife and littered the landscape with empty shells. Attempts at protecting endangered species have been successful and some wild animals are returning, including wolves, boar, gazelles, and mountain lions.

MUSIC AND DANCE

Nowhere is the colorful mixture of East and West more evident than in Lebanese music and dance. Unlike Lebanese sports, which are strictly modern, their music and dance include both traditional and modern sounds and styles.

Lebanese music is usually one of three types: traditional, fusion, or popular. Traditional music is the most Middle Eastern–sounding and can include both folk music and classical Arabic music. Often an orchestra backs a singer and includes both Eastern and Western instruments. For example, an orchestra might include Western violins, flutes, and drums and Eastern instruments such as the *oud* (a stringed instrument plucked like a guitar), *nay* (a type of flute), *dumbek* (an hourglass-shaped drum) and the *def* and the *riq* (small tambourine-like drums).

Lebanese fusion music is a blending of classical and contemporary. Some popular performers of this type include

Lebanese performer Fayrouz in a 2001 concert. Enormously popular in the 1960s, Fayrouz continues to delight audiences today.

Rabih Abou-Khalil, an oud player and composer who studied the flute in Germany and combines experimental with traditional sounds; Charbel Rouhana, an oud player and composer who combines classical sounds with New Age music; and Marcel Khalife, an oud player who has performed throughout the world and composed music for many movies and dance groups.

Lebanese popular music has grown up with the youn-ger generation in the last twenty years and has improved with age. Lebanese pop groups have enriched their sound by bringing in pianos, guitars, and drums. Some megastars have emerged in recent years, including Majida Al Roumy, a singer in her thirties who sings in classical Arabic and who calls herself "the voice of love" for Lebanon and other Arab count-ries in need; Diana Haddad, a singer in her twenties who performs in several Arabic dialects and sometimes with older popular singers; and The 4 Cats, Lebanon's first all-female pop group.

One famous Lebanese singer who is not easily categorized is Fayrouz, who began performing in the 1950s. Known as a torch singer (one who sings sentimental love songs, especially about unrequited love), she performs in many styles including jazz and flamenco. Even though she was living in Paris during the civil war, her songs inspired and comforted many Lebanese. Now in her sixties, she lives in the hills of Beirut and still performs occasionally. Her son Ziad is a well-known musician.

THE OUD

Traditional Arabic music is played on instruments that are unique to the Middle East. The most popular of these is the oud (pronounced OOD as in MOOD and sometimes spelled 'ud). The oud is a stringed instrument like a guitar, but with a shorter neck that bends back with the tuning pegs. The word oud means twig or piece of wood in Arabic. The body (sound box) of the oud is made by gluing thin tapered strips of wood edge to edge. It is flat in the front with one to three sound holes and rounded in the back. Ouds can have from two to thirteen strings, but most used today have eleven: five pairs tuned in unison and a single bass string. They are usually plucked with a metal or plastic pick or sometimes with fingers (originally they were plucked with an eagle feather). There are no frets (ridges) on the neck of the oud under the strings as there are on a guitar. This contributes to its unique sound. Many ouds are inlaid with intricate designs with some along the neck used as reference guides for placing the fingers.

The origins of the oud are not completely known. Pictures of similar instruments have been discovered in Egyptian pyramids and in Mesopotamian ruins. It was played by Persians and Indians and adopted and improved by the

Arabs in the Middle Ages. Throughout the Arab world, differences evolved in the structure and the playing of the oud. In Turkey, for example, the oud is played more delicately with a vibrating sound. In Egypt, the strings are plucked more firmly, which dulls the sound.

In medieval times, oud music was thought to have healing powers and was used to treat illnesses. It was also played on the battlefield. From Arab Spain, the oud passed into European music circles where it evolved into the lute (in Arabic, lute is *al-'ud*, meaning "of the oud").

Marcel Khalife, a popular Lebanese singer, plays an oud.

A family dances the dabke, Lebanon's national dance. Accompanied by evocative music, the dabke *interprets scenes of village life.*

Two traditional types of dance are still going strong in Lebanon. One is the *dabke*, Lebanon's national dance. A lively, five-step folk dance, it originated in the villages of the Bekaa Valley and is now performed all over the country, especially at weddings and festivals. The dancers wear traditional village costumes in bright colors. Holding hands, they move in circles, led by a master dancer in front. Accompanied by music with haunting overtones, the *dabke* illustrates stories of village life from marriages to disputes.

Although not strictly Lebanese, the centuries-old and sensual art of belly dancing is still gyrated throughout the country at many nightclubs, restaurants, and parties. Performed by women in somewhat revealing clothing, its origins are a mystery. Some think it might have been a pagan dance performed at temples—or a private and much more modest dance performed by women in harems.

Lebanon also has its own unique dance troupe—Caracalla— which performs in casinos and festivals and is very popular. The troupe actually straddles the line between dance and theater, combining elements of dance, opera, drama, and even modern literature.

THE MEDIA

For those times when the Lebanese prefer to stay at home, the country has a lively mixture of broadcast and published media. During the civil war, up to two hundred radio and fifty television stations were run by various militia groups, who battled it out on the airwaves. Now only one militia group—Hizbollah—has a television station. Although the group continues to fight with Israel across the southern border, it has become a political party as well, and uses its station—Manar—for religious programs and talk shows in Arabic.

The other six television stations have less of a political agenda and broadcast a mixture of programs in Arabic, English, and French. TeleLiban is government-owned and includes local and foreign programs and films. The privately owned stations offer newscasts, including CNN news, French game shows, dubbed Mexican soap operas, and American movies. Many show the news at different times in Arabic, English, or French. One station—the National Broadcasting Network (NBN)—combines a talk format with British and American documentaries.

Lebanese radio stations also broadcast in Arabic, English, and French. The FM stations, as in America, play mostly music, from classic rock and pop to techno and rave to older French and Arabic songs. Only a few stations are licensed to broadcast news and, like television, they often alternate languages.

Lebanon has several well-respected daily newspapers, including *Al Anwar, Al Nahar,* and *Alssafir,* published in Arabic; the *Daily Star* and the *Beirut Times,* published in English, and *L'Orient le Jour,* published in French. In addition, there are several glossy magazines published either weekly or monthly, catering to shopping, eating out, entertainment, business, and social news.

FILM AND THEATER

Lebanese filmmakers and playwrights are still suffering from the effects of the civil war, when many theaters closed and government funding was not available. Many left the country or did not work during the civil war.

Two who did continue working during the war were Maroun Baghdadi and Jocelyn Saab. Winner of an award at the Cannes Film Festival, Baghdadi's many films—*Beirut O'Beirut, Love All for the Homeland,* and *Out of Light*—deal mostly with themes of the absurdity of war and the importance of national reconciliation. Just as he was finishing a new movie, he died in 1994 at the age of forty-four after falling down a flight of stairs. Jocelyn Saab made approximately fifteen documentaries in Lebanon during the war. She pieced together footage from more than three hundred old films to produce *Once Upon a Time in Beirut,* a full-length film showing scenes in Beirut from 1914 to 1975. Even though she now lives in Paris, she has become one of Lebanon's most famous filmmakers.

Even before the war, Beirut was known as the film production center of the Arab world, partly due to its strong advertising industry which turned out many commercials. Now the industry is coming to life again, with at least two film festivals a year and four film production schools.

Popular themes for modern Lebanese movies include life during the civil war, leaving the country and returning again, and making a living. Some recent award-winning movies include Ziad Duweyri's *West Beirut,* about a teenage boy surviving the first year of the war; Mai Masri's *Children of Shatilla,* about a Palestinian refugee camp as seen through the eyes of its children; and Ghassan Shabab's *Beyrouthe Fautome,* about a militia soldier who returns to Beirut after ten years. Several female filmmakers are beginning to reveal women's stories as they unfold in the postwar years.

Lebanese playwrights are struggling even harder than filmmakers to get their work produced. Nevertheless, several theaters that regularly stage works in Arabic, English, or French have opened in Beirut. Some of the major playwrights include Roger Assaf, Jalal Khoury, and Elias Khoury. Since the end of the civil war, many newer playwrights have begun writing with a pessimistic voice as they question Lebanon's ability to solve its problems. Ziad Rahbani's *Of Dignity and Stubborn Folk* is a bleak parody of Lebanese society, and Rafik Ali Ahman's *The Bell* is a political monologue.

In a lighter vein, many urban Lebanese enjoy nightclub and cabaret acts. The Casino du Liban in Jounieh was famous before the civil war for its spectacular shows, which it is trying to revive.

LITERATURE

Lebanon's rich history has inspired many novelists and poets to put pen to paper, or in today's world, fingers to keyboard. Two of the best known are Kahlil Gibran and Amin Maalouf. Gibran was an essayist, poet, and painter who admonished his fellow citizens to throw off Turkish rule and break down religious walls. He lived most of his life in the United States and died in 1931 before Lebanon became independent.

Amin Maalouf is another expatriate who has lived in Paris since 1976 and is now in his fifties. He is known for his historical fiction, such as *The Rock of Tanios*, a love story set in early nineteenth-century Lebanon. His books have been translated into more than twenty languages.

In more recent years, several Lebanese novels have grappled with the human sides of the civil war. These include: *Sitt Marie Rose* by Etel Adnan; *Unreal City* by Tony Hananan, about a Lebanese man living in London who returns to fight with the Hizbollah; *Death in Beirut* by Tawfig Yusuf Awwad, about a Shiite village girl who comes to the city to attend college in the late 1960s (the author himself was killed by gunfire in 1989); and *Dear Mr. Kawabata*, by Rashid al-Daif, a young man's dying thoughts about his childhood village, written in the form of letters to a Japanese novelist.

Several novels by Lebanese women writers reveal their unique point of view about the civil war. *Beirut Blues*, by Hanan al-Shakn, describes a woman's life as she tries to survive in a bombarded city and revisits her childhood home in the Bekaa Valley. It too is written in the form of letters to various friends, family members, and idols (including American blues singer Billie Holiday). *The Stone of Laughter* by Huda Barakat portrays a woman who is kidnapped and then drawn into the masculine world, and *Flight Against Time* by Emily Nasrallah describes the uprooting of families. Although many Lebanese writers are tired of writing about the war, they realize they still have a need to talk about it. Emily Nasrallah describes these mixed feelings:

> Many times I tried to flee from the war so that I wouldn't keep writing about the tragedy all the time; but we are forced to do so because the war haunts us. It sucks our blood and the light of our eyes and deprives us of the basis of our existence. How can we free ourselves from it?[22]

KAHLIL GIBRAN

Although he spent more than two thirds of his life living in the United States, Kahlil Gibran, known as Jubran Khalil Jubran in the Middle East, is Lebanon's most famous writer. A novelist, poet, essayist, and painter, he is best known as the author of *The Prophet*, a collection of mystical essays he published in 1923. Since then it has been translated into twenty languages and remained a consistent bestseller.

Gibran was born on January 6, 1883, in Lebanon's northern mountain town of Bcharre. A solitary child, Gibran wandered the ruggedly beautiful countryside which would influence his later work profoundly. At the age of eight, he

fell off a cliff and dislocated his left shoulder, which caused him pain throughout his life.

In 1895 Gibran's mother emigrated to the United States, while his father remained in Lebanon. She settled in a large Syrian community in Boston with her four children, eventually saving enough money to open a family grocery store where they all worked. Gibran was sent almost immediately to a special class for immigrant children, where he was noticed by teachers for his sketching ability. Three years later, he returned to Lebanon to study Arabic literature.

A photo of Kahlil Gibran in traditional Lebanese dress

These same themes are also being voiced by many Lebanese poets, including Nour Salman, Khalil Hain, and Nadeen Nainy. Jean Said Makdisi, a Lebanese-Palestinian, ends her book *Beirut Fragments: A War Memoir* with a poem which includes the following:

Is it possible to hope that from the rubble of war, which at certain times seemed to have ended civilization, a new form might arise and permit future creativity? There is something of the alpha and the omega in this hope, is there not?[23]

In 1902 he returned to Boston and sold the family business after his mother, brother, and one of his sisters died. While his remaining sister supported him as a seamstress, he began to sketch and exhibit his charcoal drawings. At one of his exhibits he met Mary Haskell, a teacher who would become Gibran's friend, editor, and benefactor. With her encouragement, he began writing articles for local newspapers and magazines. His writing was often mystical and romantic, based on stories he had heard as a child or from the Bible.

In 1908 Gibran moved to Paris, where he took art lessons from the French painter August Rodin. His work included impressionistic landscapes and nude figures that often appeared to be floating. In 1910 he returned to the United States and moved to New York. A small, attractive man with dark hair and eyes and a compelling personality, he became a popular figure in the arts community. He drew a series of portraits of famous people, including French actress Sarah Bernhardt and Irish poet W.B. Yeats.

He also continued his writing, influenced by the styles of William Blake, an eighteenth-century English writer and artist, and Friedrich Nietzsche, a German philosopher. For his fellow Middle Easterners, he wrote in Arabic and called for revolt against the oppressive Turkish rulers and even the Maronite Church. For Westerners, he wrote in English, romanticizing his homeland and calling for peace.

Despite his success, Gibran was plagued by pain from his old shoulder injury and by anxiety and depression. He began drinking excessively and developed liver disease. He began to think about returning to his homeland, which, in some ways, he had never left. He made inquiries about buying an old monastery in Bcharre. Unfortunately, his liver disease progressed to cancer and on April 10, 1931, at the age of 48, he died.

Shortly after, Mary and his sister bought the monastery and took his body there, where he lies today surrounded by his paintings and manuscripts in the Gibran Museum.

One type of folk poetry that has been performed in Lebanon—and other Arab countries—for hundreds of years is *zajal* (pronounced TSAH-zahl). *Zajal* is performed by a group of poets, each taking a turn to improvise a witty line. Often they are sung over food and drink and taunts from the audience.

PAINTING AND SCULPTURE

Two Lebanese writers—Kahlil Gibran and Etel Adnan—are also accomplished artists. Gibran, who studied under French painter and sculptor Auguste Rodin and was strongly

DAYS OF REMEMBRANCE AND CELEBRATION

The Lebanese celebrate many special days throughout the year, including national and religious holidays. In addition to these, each village may also honor its own patron saint with a yearly parade and festival.

Lebanese national holidays include New Year's Day, January 1; Mother's Day, March 21; Labor Day, May 1; and Independence Day, November 22. In addition, two other days are set aside to remember important events: Qana Day, April 18, when 107 Lebanese were killed by Israelis at a United Nations camp in Qana in 1996; and Martyr's Day, May 6, when several Lebanese and Syrian men were hung by the Ottoman Turks in 1916 for demonstrating for independence.

For their religious holidays, Muslims follow their own calendar, which has twelve months of either twenty-nine or thirty days each. It is based on a lunar cycle in which the length of each month is determined by the time it takes the moon to rotate around the earth. This means that the Muslim calendar year is eleven days shorter than the Western one, and that their holidays fall on different days each year. It takes about thirty-three years for the whole cycle to complete.

At the beginning of their cal-

A Muslim prays in a Beirut mosque during Eid al-Fitr, which marks the end of the Ramadan fast.

influenced by British artist and writer William Blake, created more than 175 oil paintings, drawings, ink washes, and watercolors.

Adnan, who divides her time between the United States, France, and Lebanon, paints in oil and also creates ceramics and tapestries. Artist and poet Joseph Matar has held more than sixty exhibitions of his oils and watercolors throughout the world. He is known for his impressionistic landscape paintings, sometimes called sacred art. Another painter who specializes in nostalgic landscapes is David Kurani, who uses the soft edges of watercolors to romanticize images of endar years, Muslims celebrate New Year's Day (Al-Hijrah) which marks the Prophet Muhammad's flight from Mecca to Medina in A.D. 622. They also celebrate his birthday, known as Mouloud.

One of the most important Muslim events is Ramadan, celebrated in the ninth month of the Islamic calendar by fasting in the daytime and feasting at night. It is considered a holy month and a time of spiritual cleansing by Muslims and usually means spending days quietly (sometimes sleeping) and evenings in a more lively way (sometimes staying up all night). On the twenty-seventh of Ramadan, Muslims celebrate the Night of Power, when the Koran was revealed to Muhammad. At the end of Ramadan, Muslims celebrate Eid al-Fitr (Feast of Breaking the Fast). It starts on the first day of the tenth month of the Islamic calendar and lasts for four days. In preparation for the holiday, Muslims clean their houses and if they have money, they buy new clothes or furniture. They spend the four days enjoying large meals with as many members of their family as they can.

The Lebanese Christians celebrate Easter in March or April with holidays on Good Friday, Easter Sunday, and Easter Monday. The Orthodox and Catholic Easters are celebrated a week apart. There are processions through the streets, starting on Palm Sunday when families and children carry palm branches and candles to church. On Easter Sunday a priest leads another procession to an unlighted church and knocks three times before being admitted.

Christmas Day, December 25, is celebrated much as it is in Western countries, with family reunions, the exchanging of gifts around decorated trees, and church service, including midnight mass. Santa Claus is called Papa Noel by some Lebanese. Armenian Christians, who make up 5 percent of Lebanon's population, celebrate Christmas on January 6. Some Christians also celebrate January 6 as the Epiphany, the manifestation of the divinity of Jesus. They make special Epiphany cakes shaped like fingers.

Lebanon. Amin al-Basha is known among art critics as the artist who likes to illustrate everyday life. One of his most recent exhibits featured a group of small wooden paintings attached together in a frame. Some artists, like Munir Najem, combine Eastern with Western art. His recent murals and oil paintings use rich blues and greens and incorporate themes from Arabian folktales. Other well-known Lebanese artists include Hassan Jouni, Moustafa Farroukh, Mohammad Rawas, and Marwan Rechmawi.

The most famous Lebanese sculptors are the Basbous brothers—Michel, Yusef and Alfred—whose work lines the streets in Rachana, an artistic community they created in the Mount Lebanon area north of Byblos. Before Michel died in 1981 he built a unique house using a variety of found objects, such as car parts. Today it is used by Yusef as a workshop. Both he and his brother Alfred, who works nearby, make primitive figures out of wood, stone, and metal.

Sculptor Nadine Abu Zaki recently exhibited a rose-colored marble and stone work called *Towers of Silence.* Carved as two columns of vertical blocks rising side by side, they are seen by some as a symbolic tribute to those who died in the September 11 attack on the World Trade Center in New York. Zaki, who has studied philosophy and theology, says that her columns are "towers of strength" and represent "spiritual ascension and the search for inner silence."[24]

FOLK ARTS

Many of the traditional handicrafts in Lebanon have been replaced by mass-produced goods. Glassmaking, once a thriving Phoenician art, has moved east to Damascus. Some artisans are still at work, however: men with metals and women with weaving and embroidery. Metalwork includes inlaying softer metals into harder ones, especially copper and brass, and carving intricate designs, mostly of Turkish origin. This practice of beautifying less expensive metals evolved when the Prophet Muhammad banned the use of gold and silver because he thought it was too extravagant. In some souks men can still be seen pulling fine gold wire to make filigree jewelry. In the country and in the Palestinian refugee camps, many women embroider linen, cotton, and lace. Even living in the harshest of conditions, these women sew beautifully patterned colors into pillows and clothing and other items that are sold around the world. Like many Lebanese, they are still far too close to the recent devastation of war, but determined anyway to celebrate life in as many ways as they can.

REBUILDING FOR THE TWENTY-FIRST CENTURY

7

It has been over a decade since Lebanon's civil war ended. Since then, most warring factions have put down their arms, crossed the Green Line, and gotten to work cleaning up the damage. The Lebanese consider themselves a resourceful people and they have made remarkable progress in just a few years. In the years ahead, however, they will continue to face many more severe challenges—both internally and externally. Within their borders, they must work to build a strong and peaceful country. Beyond their borders, they must help their warring neighbors end violence and negotiate peace. If they are going to survive and thrive in this new century, they will have to call upon every bit of their resourceful character.

A Strong Government for a Strong Country

One of the reasons that civil war tore Lebanon apart is that its government was not strong enough to hold the country together. It was a structure designed to work in theory that did not work in reality. People still identified with their religious groups more than they did with the idea of a democratic nation.

The 1989 Taif Accord (Charter of National Reconciliation) was an attempt to change this. Drawn up in Taif, Saudi Arabia, by the Arab League nations, it called for government re-forms such as representing people more fairly in their districts and balancing the power of the president with that of the prime minister. While these changes did allow more Shiite Muslims to be represented (one of the shortcomings of the prior government), not all Lebanese are happy with these changes. According to Lebanese journalist Carole Dagher, warring militias saw the Taif Accord as a necessary evil which required them to put down their arms in exchange for government office.

Former Prime Minister Rafia Hariri (center) votes in a 2000 election. The future of Lebanon depends on a strong government to unite its diverse population.

Others believe it is a transition to a secular form of government—one not based on religious representation. Realistically, this transition is unlikely to happen anytime soon. The different religious groups in Lebanon still live separately from one another and many are resistant to change. To Muslims, the idea of the separation of church and state is unthinkable. Some Christians, fearing an Islamic fundamentalist takeover, are leaving the country. Participating in the political process is still an alien idea to many: Only 55 percent of Lebanese voted in the 1998 elections.

Some Lebanese think there should be more open dialogue between different groups, guided by a stronger sense of Lebanese identity. Yet this idea still meets with resistance.

Many think it is a waste of time because open dialogue has not prevented war in the past. They also are cynical about their government's bureaucratic inefficiencies and corruption and its overreliance on foreign powers. Real progress is more likely to evolve slowly and naturally. Fortunately several civil, educational, business, and labor groups are working hard to bring about changes at a grassroots level. Lebanon's future—and that of the Middle East—depends on it.

ECONOMY

When the civil war ended, Lebanon was bankrupt, Beirut's reputation as a hub of Arab wealth a distant memory. Many people were homeless; most were jobless. During the 1990s the government undertook ambitious rebuilding plans. With the help of loans from the World Bank, the European Union, and other Arab states, Prime Minister Rafiq Hariri set up the Council for Development and Reconstruction, a ten-year,

In the 1990s the Lebanese government invested heavily in a program to rebuild infrastructure and buildings like this mosque destroyed during the war.

HIZBOLLAH

One group that has worked to rebuild Lebanon—and its own image—is Hizbollah. Called the "Party of God," it was founded in 1982 as a radical Shiite Muslim organization from a loose coalition of Shiite groups supported by Iran and Syria. Originally calling themselves a resistance group, they flew the Lebanese flag during the Israeli occupation and promoted conversion to Islam. They claimed responsibility for bombing the American embassy and marine headquarters in Beirut in 1983 and for kidnapping Western hostages. The group now plays down its terrorist tactics and blames these on its umbrella militias, Islamic Jihad and Hamas.

Since the civil war, Hizbollah has evolved into a powerful political group of about five thousand members with a more moderate agenda and a friendly image. They have raised money for housing, education, and health care and in 1992 won twelve seats in Parliament. They have their own television station. They were the only militia to retain arms after the civil war and they continue to exchange fire with the Israelis across the southern border.

To many poor Shiites in Lebanon, Hizbollah represents their first organized voice. In the southern city of Tyre, there is a Hizbollah souvenir shop selling items like T-shirts and calendars with the Hizbollah logo.

$18.1 billion plan to rebuild the country's infrastructure. A private company—Solidere—formed to rebuild Beirut's downtown area. Although Beirut has undergone an amazing rebirth, there is still much work to do. The government is now spending more money on other parts of Lebanon and several buildings in Beirut are still unfinished.

After a brief boom, the economy slowed down and current president Emile Lahoud is sticking to a tight budget, aimed in part at paying off immense debt (up to 40 percent of the budget). It has not been easy for the government to implement reforms and curb spending at the same time. The unemployment rate is still high (18 percent and up to 30 percent for young people) and the gap between rich and poor continues to widen. Several parts of the country are still unstable as people displaced by the war are settling into new communities or returning to old ones. Many Lebanese resent the cheap labor imported from surrounding countries, especially Syria. Farmers are feeling the competition from Syrian imports although grape and potato crops are making a comeback.

The economic future does not look good, according to political analysts Steven N. Simon and Jonathan Stevenson's article in the *World Policy Journal*:

> There are wide income disparities between rich and poor in Lebanon, and the middle class is beleaguered. The Lebanese tend to regard their government as . . . incompetent and corrupt. . . . The government's cumulative deficit exceeds $22 billion . . . and is growing. Debt service consistently sucks out over 90 percent of government revenues and exceeded 100 percent in July 2000. Lebanon's 2001 budget calls for a deficit equal to

An Australian couple shares a nargileh by the sea in Beirut. Tourism is playing a key role in Lebanon's economic recovery.

more than half of its public expenditure, and its sovereign debt rating—sub-investment grade to begin with—has been lowered. The country experienced zero growth in 2000.[25]

Despite these drawbacks, there are some encouraging economic signs and the Lebanese are highly motivated to achieve financial success. With few natural resources (such as oil), they are used to relying on their business ability. Worldwide, they have an excellent reputation for repaying their debts. The Lebanese pound has remained stable. The stock market reopened in 1996. The banking system is financially sound and many small and medium-sized manufacturing industries are up and running, including metal fabricating, textiles, oil refining, and food production. Jobs have been gradually increasing (1.3 million Lebanese are in the labor force) as businesses reopen in private hands. Tourism, which before the war accounted for 20 percent of

 ## THE PROCESS OF RECOVERY

According to Lebanese philosophy professor Elizabeth Kassab, the Lebanese remain torn between the wish to forget their war experiences and the need to communicate them to others. In her opinion, the process of recovery is ongoing as the Lebanese work to overcome their psychological wounds and feelings of isolation from the rest of the world. It also requires honest self-examination, as she writes in her article "The Paramount Reality of the Beirutis":

> The war started and ended without the explicit will of most of us, but fed on our fears, wishes and dreams. Now it is time to examine these together if we wish to become less vulnerable to the demons of collective aggression and collective suicide. It is time to set up civil forums of debate about our past, our present and our future. It is also time to cry out our wounds and our fears. We live in a region where ethnic and religious conflicts have caused cumulative injuries throughout the ages, and Lebanon seems to have inherited most of them, with Beirut as their epitome. Unless we are honest about our fear and fantasies, we won't be able to take the first step towards reinstating democracy. The biggest challenge to Lebanon today is to move the ancient and recent wounds of its different groups to the democratic duty of mutual respect and understanding. This is something that no one else will do for us. It is in our vital interest to do it as properly and as thoroughly as we can. We are the guardians of the ruins but also the builders of the future.

the national income, is growing at a rate of 10 percent a year, bolstered by new hotels and restaurants, an expanded airport, and a new six-lane freeway into Beirut.

Population Shifts

One of the government's priorities, besides rebuilding the economy and the infrastructure, is finding homes for everyone. A new department was created specifically for this purpose, called the Ministry of Displaced. Today few Lebanese are without homes, but for many, homes are makeshift squatter settlements outside the cities or bombed-out buildings in the slums of the cities. In recent years more and more Lebanese have moved into the cities to find jobs. In fact, many of the country's approximately 3.6 million people have moved, creating new communities and rearranging the demographic map.

Exact numbers are impossible to pinpoint because there has been no public census in Lebanon since 1932. It is estimated, however, that from 125,000 to 150,000 died in the civil war and 1.5 million—half the population—were left homeless. Approximately 500,000 left the country and 15,000 are still unaccounted for or missing. Since the war ended in 1990, about 40,000 have returned.

Another major population shift has been the increase of Muslims to about 70 percent of the population and the decline of Christians to about 30 percent. More Christians than Muslims are emigrating to other countries, fearing the anti-Western sentiments of some Muslims. Many Lebanese fear that if this trend continues, Lebanon's unique identity as a multicultural Arab country will disappear.

Health Care

Although Lebanon has one of the best health care systems in the Middle East, the civil war undermined health in general for everyone in the country. In addition to devastating physical injuries, people have had to endure homelessness, hunger, mental trauma, and polluted air and water. Today most basic services such as sewer systems, running water, and garbage collection have been restored, but pollution remains a problem. The Lebanese suffer from a high rate of deaths due to upper respiratory and lower intestinal tract disorders.

PROTECTING LEBANON'S FRAGILE ENVIRONMENT

Part of rebuilding Lebanon is protecting its natural assets and wildlife. Although many of these, from the famous cedar trees to wolves and turtles, are endangered, many efforts are being made to conserve and improve what is left. These efforts include three nature reserves run by the government, awareness campaigns sponsored by volunteer organizations, and environmental tourism promoted by private entrepreneurs.

Lebanon's three nature reserves are run by the Department of the Ministry with money from the government and private organizations, both local and international. They include the Chouf Cedar Reserve, the Horsh Ehden Nature Reserve, and the Palm Islands Reserve. The largest is the Chouf Cedar Reserve with more than 123,000 acres of cedar forests. It is located partly in the Chouf Mountains southeast of Beirut and partly in the Bekaa Valley. Some of the cedars are thought to be up two thousand years old. The reserve also attracts more than two hundred species of birds and twenty-six species of wild mammals, including wolves, gazelles, and wild boar.

The Horsh Ehden Nature Reserve protects what is most like Lebanon's ancient forests, including cedar, juniper, fir, and wild apple trees; the Lebanese violet; and rare birds and butterflies. In addition, it includes many small mammals such as squirrel, weasel, badger, wolves, and hyenas. In recent years wild boars have become a problem, increasing in number and eating the protected plant life. Although no hunting is allowed in any of the reserves, the management is thinking of making an exception in this case and allowing the boars to be hunted. The reserve

Partly because of the interruptions of the civil war, there are very few health records and thus little information on rates of certain diseases. The overall level of health is fair to average, with an infant mortality rate of 17 deaths in every 1000 births, compared to 7 for every 1000 in the United States, and an average lifespan of 74 years, compared to 76 in the United States. The rate of HIV/AIDS (.09 percent) is low compared to many parts of the world.

For the poor people in Lebanon, health care is too expensive and requires insurance, but the general level of care available is good. Many doctors are trained in the United States or in France. Although there are several major hospitals, there is no ambulance service. People in need of emergency help must rely on Red Cross volunteers.

covers ten square miles in the north part of Mount Lebanon, about twenty miles east of Tripoli. Just off the coast from Tripoli lies Palm Islands Reserve, which includes three islands in a three-square-mile area. Designated a protected area in 1992 by United Nations Educational, Scientific and Cultural Organization (UNESCO), it offers a safe haven for Mediterranean green turtles, monk seals, and migratory birds.

In addition to these government-run reserves, many volunteer organizations in Lebanon are working hard to promote awareness of the environment and the detrimental effects of industrial pollution, use of pesticides, and overbuilding. These include Greenpeace and GreenLine. Formed in 1991 by teachers and students at the American University of Beirut, GreenLine has helped keep the last public beaches away from private developers and organizes treks into the countryside to promote environmental awareness.

Two enterprising businessmen in Lebanon are making money and protecting the environment at the same time. They run the Al-Jord Ecolodge, a community in the remote northern part of the Lebanon Mountains. Visitors can stay in stone huts or tents and take long or short hikes, ride mountain bikes, climb rocks, or explore caves. At the same time, they can learn about the environment and the history of the area and volunteer to plant trees. According to Lonely Planet travel writers Siona Jenkins and Ann Jousiffe in *Lebanon*: "The company is on a mission to bring prosperity to the area's depressed economy while at the same time preserving its environmental and cultural resources."

THE ENVIRONMENT

The health of Lebanon's environment also suffered as a result of the war. Even before the war, it was in fragile condition. The once dense forests of cedar and other trees have been cut down and now cover only a small amount of land. Illegal mining, too many cars, overuse of pesticides, and unplanned development have all further damaged land, water, and air. The civil war delivered the final blow: tearing up the land with bombs and mines, and littering it with waste and garbage.

In the last decade much of the garbage has been cleaned up and buried in landfills. There are still no waste treatment plants and much of the sewage spills out into the sea, making the beaches unusable. Ironically, the beaches in southern

A man who has scavenged a pair of crates walks along a Beirut beach ruined by war and pollution. Lebanon's environment was ravaged by the civil war.

Lebanon have been saved—but only because the area is filled with unexploded land mines from the war. Many Lebanese fear that once the land mines are cleared, uncontrolled high-rise development will continue to deny access to the beach for the majority of people, as has happened around Beirut.

In an attempt to clean up urban and agricultural areas, both government and nongovernment groups have launched educational campaigns. Some of Lebanon's resources are being protected in three nature reserves: the Chouf Cedar Reserve, the Horsh Ehden Nature Reserve, and the Palm Islands Reserve. In addition, some resourceful Lebanese are promoting an environmentally friendly tourist industry.

BEYOND THE BORDERS

Many of the challenges Lebanon faces in this new century extend beyond its borders. The Israelis continue fighting with the Palestinians nearby and with the Hizbollah militia across the southern border. For the Lebanese, this is too close for comfort and they fear another invasion. The Syrians are everywhere. At this point in their history, after surviving at least twelve conquerors and countless meddlers, the Lebanese have a strong desire to be left alone. Like it or not, however, they are being made to pay attention to their neighbors—and consequently to play an important role in Middle Eastern politics.

THE FATE OF THE PALESTINIAN REFUGEES

Although the warring Israeli and Palestinian forces have left Lebanon, they continue to attack each other in other areas. Many countries in the Middle East—and indeed the world—fear an all-out war that will cause even more death and destruction. They would like to see an end to this conflict that has been blazing for more than fifty years.

In March 2002 the Lebanese hosted an Arab League summit in Beirut. During this summit, Crown Prince Abdullah of Saudi Arabia presented a peace initiative, reintroducing the "land for peace" resolution—that Israel exchange the Palestinian land it

Saudi Crown Prince Abdullah (center) takes part in a 2002 Arab Summit in Beirut. Lebanon plays an important role in Middle Eastern politics.

is occupying for the right to exist in peace. Even though the Israelis did not attend and the Palestinians walked out halfway through, the summit was seen as a positive step. For the first time in fifty years, Arabs were able to agree on a unified charter of principles and course of action and to recognize the existence of Israel as a state. Leaders are hopeful that the Palestinians and the Israelis will both be able to compromise and that a "two-state solution" will work. Then the 1.1 million Palestinians living in refugee camps (350,000 in Lebanon) will at last have a state of their own and be able to leave Lebanon. Although the Lebanese are sympathetic toward the Palestinians, they do not want them to stay in Lebanon, mostly because they would upset the balance of power.

SOUTHERN LANDS AND WATERS

After overstaying their unwelcome occupation by two decades, the Israelis finally withdrew from southern Lebanon in the spring of 2000. Most of the South Lebanese Army (SLA) they had trained, considered traitors by the Lebanese, went with them. The border is closed, now patrolled by a United Nations interim force of about 3,600 soldiers and 450 civilians. It is sometimes referred to as the Blue Line.

Although the Israeli solders are gone, they are not forgotten. They watch from several observation towers they have built along the border. The towers were built to help keep Israel safe, but ironically they have had the opposite effect—provoking attacks from Hizbollah guerillas. Villages on both sides of the Blue Line are shelled almost daily; several soldiers on both sides have been captured. The Lebanese fear that this shelling will escalate into another Israeli invasion and have called for a disbanding of the Hizbollah militia, the only one that did not turn in its arms after the civil war.

One particular hot spot in this area is Golan Heights, located where the borders of Lebanon, Israel, and Syria meet. Originally part of Syria, it was captured and taken over by Israel during the 1967 war. The Lebanese claim that part of it is their land, although the United Nations disagrees. It is in this area that a tributary of the Hasbani River (a tributary of the Jordan River) comes within a few miles of Lebanon's Litani River. The Israelis accuse the Lebanese and Syrians of destroying their water-diversion projects from the Hasbani

River. The Lebanese accuse the Israelis of diverting water through underground tunnels from the Litani River. Both countries argue about who needs the water more. Lebanon uses the river for about 35 percent of its electricity and is the only country in the region with self-sustaining water resources. Israel has almost depleted its water resources, but has more advanced technical resources to develop other ways of getting water, such as recycling and desalination (removing salt to make water drinkable). It is possible that if the fighting over these border lands and waters ever stops, both Israel and Lebanon could benefit by sharing the river and technology.

Syrian army officers direct traffic in a Beirut neighborhood. Many Lebanese resent the lingering Syrian presence in their country.

THE SYRIANS

Another neighbor—the Syrians to the north and east—is also far too close for the comfort of many Lebanese. Although some Syrian troops withdrew in 2001, approximately twenty-five thousand remain in Lebanon. Syrian workers and products are everywhere. In addition, the Syrians are funding and arming the Hizbollah militia in an

effort to keep Israel on alert. Many Lebanese—especially
the Christians and Druze—want the Syrians to leave and
have demonstrated against them. The Syrians reply that
they are still there because the Lebanese government wants
them to be and because the Lebanese Armed Forces is too
weak. In their opinion, Lebanon has yet to implement all
the reforms required by the Taif Accord, which also calls for
Syrian withdrawal.

Like their ancestors the Phoenicians, the Lebanese are
facing unknown waters as they navigate their country into
a new century. Hopefully they are moving away from violence and toward a peaceful new0 world. As historian
Bernard Lewis describes it, Lebanon could became part of
a new holy war which might engulf the whole Middle East,
or it could unite with its neighbors and the world for peace
and sharing of resources:

> For the moment, the outside world seems disposed to
> leave them in peace, and perhaps even to help them
> achieve it. They alone—the peoples and governments
> of the Middle East—can decide whether and how to use
> this window of opportunity while, in an interval of their
> troubled modern history, it remains open.[26]

Facts About Lebanon

General Information

Official name: Republic of Lebanon

Type of government: parliamentary republic with unicameral legislature, National Assembly; 128 members elected by popular vote on basis of sectarian proportional representation; speaker of the legislature must be a Shiite Muslim

Chief of state: president, elected by National Assembly; must be a Maronite Christian

Head of government: prime minister, appointed by the president in consultation with the National Assembly; must be a Sunni Muslim

Capital: Beirut

Major cities: Tarabulus (Tripoli), Zahle, Saida (Sidon), Sur (Tyre)

Official language: Arabic

Other languages: English, French

Monetary unit: Lebanese pound

Exchange rate (2001): 1.514 = 1$ U.S.

People

Population (2001): 3.6 million

Population growth rate: 1.38%

Density: persons per square mile, 884

Population distribution (2000): urban, 90%; rural, 10%

Population by age: under 15, 27.5%; 15–64, 65.7%; 65 and over, 6.7%

Ethnic composition: Arabic, 94%; Armenian, 5%; other, 1%

Official religion: none

Religious affiliation: Islamic, including Druze, Sunni, and Shiite, 70%; Christian, including Maronite, Greek Catholic, Greek Orthodox, 30%

Vital Statistics

Birth rate per 1,000 population (1998): 27

Death rate per 1,000 population (1998): 7

Infant mortality rate per 1,000 live births (2002): 17

Total fertility rate (average births per childbearing woman (2000)): 2

Life expectancy at birth (2000): 74

SOCIAL INDICATORS

Literacy age 15 and over (1997): total population, 86.4%; male, 90.8%; female, 82.2%

Political participation: Eligible voters participating in last national election (1998): 55%. Voting is compulsory for all males 21 and over; women must have elementary education to vote

Working life (1996–97): labor force, 1.3 million; 1 million foreign workers; employed in agriculture, 7%; business and industry, 31%; services, 62%; unemployed, 18%

ECONOMY

Gross domestic product (2000): $18.2 billion, $5,000 per capita

Annual growth rate (1990–99): 5.7%

Budget revenue (2000): $3.31 billion

Expenditures: $5.5 billion

Inflation rate (1990–99): 24% per year

Major export destinations: Saudi Arabia, UAE, Syria. Exports: $700 million (agricultural products, chemicals, textiles, metals, and jewelry)

Major import sources: Italy, Syria, France, Germany, United States

NOTES

INTRODUCTION: LEBANON: CAUGHT IN THE CROSSFIRE

1. Robert Fisk, *Pity the Nation: The Abduction of Lebanon.* New York: Atheneum, 1990, p. 163.

CHAPTER 1: BIGGER THAN ITS BORDERS

2. Richard Covington, "Beirut Rises from the Ashes," *Smithsonian,* April 2000.

CHAPTER 2: THE DIVERSE PEOPLE OF LEBANON

3. Kamal Salibi, *The Modern History of Lebanon.* New York: Caravan Books, 1996, p. xxvi.

4. Salibi, *The Modern History of Lebanon,* p. xxvii.

CHAPTER 3: A LINK BETWEEN EMPIRES

5. Salibi, *The Modern History of Lebanon,* p. 5.

6. Salibi, *The Modern History of Lebanon,* p. 16.

7. Salibi, The *Modern History of Lebanon,* p. 79.

8 Kamal Salibi, *A House of Many Mansions: The History of Lebanon Reconsidered.* Berkeley: University of California Press, 1988, p. 69.

CHAPTER 4: IN SEARCH OF A MODERN IDENTITY

9. Salibi, *A House of Many Mansions,* p. 191.

10. Fisk, *Pity the Nation,* p. 278.

11. Thomas Friedman, *From Beirut to Jerusalem.* New York: Farrar, Straus and Giroux, 1989, p. 233.

12. Friedman, *From Beirut to Jerusalem,* p. 30.

CHAPTER 5: THE SHIFTING PATTERNS OF DAILY LIFE

13. Dorothy Stannard, ed., *Syria and Lebanon*. London: Insight Guides, 2000, p. 256.

14. Covington, "Beirut Rises from the Ashes."

15. Siona Jenkins and Ann Jousiffe, *Lebanon*. Oakland, CA: Lonely Planet, 2001, p. 199.

16. Marilyn Raschka, "Re-Rooting Lebanon's War-Displaced Farmers," *Washington Report on Middle East Affairs*, August/September 1997. www.washington-report.org.

17. William Harris, *Faces of Lebanon: Sects, Wars, and Global Extensions*. Princeton: Markus Wiener, 1997, p. 75.

18. Covington, "Beirut Rises from the Ashes."

19. Borre Ludvigsen, "Reflections on a Trip to Lebanon 1995," *Al Mashriq (The Levant)*. http://almashriq.hiof.no/lebanon.

CHAPTER 6: CELEBRATING LIFE WITH ARTS AND ENTERTAINMENT

20. Jenkins and Jousiffe, *Lebanon*, p. 91.

21. Jenkins and Jousiffe, *Lebanon*, p. 104.

22. Quoted in Elizabeth Kassab, "The Paramount Reality of the Beirutis: War Literature and the Lebanese Conflict," *Lebanese Center for Policy Studies*. www.lcps-lebanon.org.

23. Jean Said Makdisi, excerpts from *Beirut Fragments: A War Memoir, Al Mashriq (The Levant)*. Book reprinted on http://almashriq.hiof.no/lebanon.

24. Quoted in Farida Khizan, "Sculpture Exhibit Reaches for New Heights," *Daily Star Online*, April 2002. www.dailystar.com.

CHAPTER 7: REBUILDING FOR THE TWENTY-FIRST CENTURY

25. Steven N. Simon and Jonathan Stevenson, "Declawing the Party of God: Toward Normalization in Lebanon," *World Policy Journal*, Summer 2001.

26. Bernard Lewis, *The Middle East: A Brief History of the Last 2,000 Years*. New York: Scribner, 1996, p. 387.

GLOSSARY

Amal: Shiite militia which is now a political party.

Blue Line: The border between Lebanon and Israel.

Chador: A black garment worn by Muslim women. Also called a *hejab*.

Confessionalism: Political representation based on religious sects.

Druze: A sect of Islam that originated in the eleventh century in Egypt.

Green Line: Line which divided Beirut during the civil war from 1976 to 1991. On the east was the Christian side; on the west, the Muslim side.

Hizbollah: Radical Shiite political party. Its militia—Islamic Jihad—claimed responsibility for kidnappings during the civil war and for expelling the Israelis from south Lebanon. They continue to spar with the Israelis along the Blue Line.

hunter-gatherers: Nomadic humans who rely on hunting wild animals and gathering food to survive.

Koran: The holy book of Islam (also spelled Qur'an).

Levant: The area of the eastern Mediterranean from Egypt to Greece, including Lebanon, Syria, and Turkey. From the Greek, means "where the sun rises."

Lubnan: Arabic name for Lebanon. From Semitic root, meaning "white."

Maronites: A Christian sect established in the fifth century in Syria and which moved into the Lebanon Mountains in the seventh century.

Melchites: Greek Catholics who brought their own rites from the Eastern Roman Empire to Lebanon in the fifth century.

mazza: A variety of hot and cold food served as appetizers, including bean dips, pickled vegetables, spicy salads, meats (meatballs, sausage rolls, stuffed grape leaves), and flat bread.

nargileh: A water pipe often smoked in restaurants and cafés. Also called hubble-bubble pipe because of the sound it makes while being smoked.

nay: A type of flute.

Phalange: Christian paramilitary organization founded in 1937.

PLO: Palestinian Liberation Organization founded in 1964 to support the cause of Palestinian refugees.

Ramadan: Holy month of fasting celebrated by Muslims.

Semitic: Belonging to a group of people—the Semites—from southwestern Asia, mainly represented by the Arabs and the Jews. In ancient times, Semites were also Babylonians, Assyrians, Canaanites, and Phoenicians.

Shiism: A branch of Islam which began to form shortly after Mohammed died in A.D. 632. Shiites believe that the Prophet Muhammad's cousin Ali and his descendants are the true successors.

SLA: South Lebanese Army. A group of Lebanese, mostly Christians, recruited and trained by Israel to fight in 1978 during the civil war and to participate in the occupation of south Lebanon. They dispersed in the spring of 2000 when Israel withdrew; many fled into Israel.

souk: A market (also spelled suq).

Sunni: Main sect of Islam based on the teachings of the Prophet Muhammad (A.D. 570–632).

wadi: a gorge.

CHRONOLOGY

10,000–5000 B.C.
Humans begin to cultivate wild cereals which grew in the eastern Mediterranean and to domesticate animals, thus evolving from nomadic hunter-gatherers to settled farmers.

5000–1500 B.C.
Early Semitic people called Canaanites begin to form small villages along the coast, develop governments, sea trade and navigation, glass-making, and metal tools.

1490–36 B.C.
Egyptian pharaoh Thutmose III invades Canaan and incorporates it into the Egyptian Empire.

1100–800 B.C.
Canaanites regain dependence and flourish. Known as Phoenicians, they establish colonies throughout the Mediterranean and trade routes to Europe, Africa, and Asia.

875–608 B.C.
Assyrians invade and rule.

573–539 B.C.
Babylonians invade and rule.

539–333 B.C.
Persia invades and rules.

333–64 B.C.
Alexander the Great of Macedonia (Greece) invades. Phoenicia becomes part of the Greek Empire.

64 B.C.–A.D. 395
General Pompey invades, making Phoenicia part of the vast Roman Empire. The coastal cities, mountains, and desert in the east are governed as one province called Syria, which includes present-day Lebanon. Christianity becomes an accepted religion.

395
Roman Empire divides into two parts: Western, with capital
at Rome, and Eastern or Byzantine, with capital at Constantinople (in Turkey). Syria/Lebanon becomes part of Byzantine Empire.

500–600
Series of earthquakes demolishes temples at Baalbek and
destroys Beirut, killing nearly thirty thousand people.

570
Prophet Muhammad, founder of Islam, born in Mecca,
Arabia.

643–750
Muslim Arabs defeat local Byzantine rulers and occupy
Syria as part of Umayyad dynasty, based in Damascus.

750–1258
The Abbasids replace the Umayyads as ruling dynasty and
move capital to Baghdad. Lebanon Mountains become a
refuge for various ethnic and religious groups, including
Maronite Christians, Greek Catholics, and Druze Muslims.

1095–1291
The crusaders from Europe launch six campaigns to recap-
ture holy land from Muslims. They build towers, castles,
and churches and bring Maronites into union with Vatican.
France becomes interested in region.

1260–1516
Mamluks (former Egyptian slaves from Black and Caspian
Sea areas) take over Egypt and Syria.

1516–1916
Ottoman Turks (Central Asian people who had been Egypt-
ian slaves) incorporate Syria into Ottoman Empire. Rule
Greater Syria as a semiautonomous state through two pow-
erful Druze feudal families. Greater Syria includes Lebanon,
Syria, Jordan, and Israel.

1914–1918
Ottomans side with Germany, Austria-Hungary, and Bulgaria to fight Britain, France, Russia, and the United States in World War I. Defeated in 1918 when British move into Palestine.

1920
French given mandate over Greater Syria. Greater Lebanon established with present boundaries and Beirut as capital.

1926
First constitution drafted.

1932
First census establishes foundation for present system of selecting political officers, based on religious sects.

1940–1945
French Nazi government occupies briefly during World War II until General Charles de Gaulle visits Lebanon in 1941. Coast used as staging area during war.

1943
France transfers power on November 22. Celebrated as official Independence Day.

1945
Lebanon becomes a member of the League of Arab States and of the United Nations.

1967
War between Israel and Arab nations. Palestinian guerrilla groups start using Lebanon as a base of operations.

1968
Israelis launch raid on Beirut International Airport.

1975–1990
Civil war between more than forty Christian and Muslim militias and between Israel and the Palestinians. Israel invades Lebanon in 1982.

1989
Lebanon signs Taif Accord, known as the Charter of
Lebanese National Reconciliation.

1991
Lebanon signs Treaty of Brotherhood with Syria. All militias
except Hizbollah disbanded.

1992
First election in twenty years is held.

1996
Israel bombs Hizbollah militia bases in southern Lebanon
and attacks a UN peacekeeping base, killing more than one
hundred civilians.

1998
Emile Lahoud, commander in chief of the army, is elected
president. Salim el-Hoss is elected prime minister but later
resigns and is replaced by former Prime Minister Rafiq
Hariri, a rich businessman who has overseen much of
Beirut's reconstruction.

2000
Israel withdraws troops from security zone in southern
Lebanon.

2002
Lebanon hosts Arab League Summit.

SUGGESTIONS FOR FURTHER READING

BOOKS

Daniel Abebe, *Lebanon in Pictures*. Minneapolis: Random, 2000. Basic information about the country.

Rashid al-Daif, *Dear Mr. Kawabata*. Trans. Paul Starkey. London: Quartet Books, 1999. A novel-memoir about the Lebanese civil war written in the form of letters to a dead Japanese novelist.

Oriana Fallaci, *Inshallah*. New York: Doubleday, 1991. An Italian journalist, Fallaci has written a multicharacter novel about the civil war.

Florence Parry Heide and Judith Heide Gilliland, *Sami and the Time of the Troubles*. New York: Clarion Books, 1992. The story of a young boy and his family coping with life during the civil war.

Roseanne Khalaf, *Once Upon a Time in Lebanon*. Caravan Books, 1982. Three folk tales about Lebanese culture.

Lebanon in Pictures. Minneapolis: Lerner, 1988. Basic information about the country with many interesting pictures.

Hanan al-Shaykh, *Beirut Blues*. Trans. Catherine Cobham. New York: Anchor Books, 1995. A novel about a woman trying to make sense of her life in war-torn Beirut.

Sean Sheehan, *Lebanon*. New York: Marshall Cavendish, 1997. A well-written and thorough coverage of the culture of Lebanon, lavishly illustrated with color photographs.

WEBSITES

Beirut Times (www.beiruttimes.com): Articles from the daily newspaper.

Embassy of Lebanon (www.lebanonembassy.org). Statistical and business information about Lebanon, as well as extensive links to Lebanese media, government departments, universities, culture, food, and sports sites.

Encyclopaedia of the Orient (http://lexiorient.com). More than seven hundred terms defined from Abbas to Zionism.

GreenLine (http://greenline.org.lb). An environmental activist and educational organization founded by students and teachers at the American University of Beirut in 1991. Current campaigns include cleaning up toxic waste, preventing dredging of sand along the coast, supporting hunting legislation, and preserving and replanting forests.

International Festival (http://www.baalbeck.org.lb). Information on the yearly music festival held in August in Baalbeck.

Lebanese American Association Newsletter (www.laa.org). Information about Lebanon published three times a year for Lebanese living in the United States.

Lebanon.com (www.lebanon.com). A business- and tourist-oriented site, with links to other sites about Lebanon.

Middle East Football (www.middleeastfootball.com). Current and historical articles about football (soccer) in the Middle East, including Lebanon.

Music of Lebanon (www.musicoflebanon.com). A wide sampling of Lebanese music, top-twenty hits, album reviews, and soundtracks to download.

WORKS CONSULTED

BOOKS

Carole H. Dagher, *Bring Down the Walls: Lebanon's Post-War Challenge.* New York: St. Martin's Press, 2000. Examines the Christian-Muslim conflicts that have shaped Lebanon and the prospects for peace. Dagher is a Lebanese journalist.

Jared Diamond, *Guns, Germs, and Steel: The Fates of Human Societies.* New York: W.W. Norton and Company, 1999. Addresses the question of why history developed differently in different parts of the world and the importance of the Fertile Crescent, which includes the area that is now Lebanon. Winner of the Pulitzer Prize and highly readable.

Robert Fisk, *Pity the Nation: The Abduction of Lebanon.* New York: Atheneum, 1990. A moving, engrossing account of the civil war years in Lebanon. As a foreign correspondent for the London *Times,* Fisk lived in Beirut during the Israeli siege and was one of four Western correspondents to stay on in Lebanon after Westerners became the target for assassination and kidnapping.

Thomas Friedman, *From Beirut to Jerusalem.* New York: Farrar, Straus and Giroux, 1989. A clear and vivid of account of the Lebanese civil war and of the political situation in the Middle East, including Israeli-Palestinian relations, terrorism, and fundamentalism.

Kahlil Gibran, *Mirrors of the Soul.* Trans. Joseph Sheban. New York: Philosophical Library, 1965. A compilation of poems, essay segments, and information about Gibran's work and life.

William Harris, *Faces of Lebanon: Sects, Wars, and Global Extensions.* Princeton: Markus Wiener, 1997. An analysis of the "Lebanonization" of Lebanon and its place in the world, especially since the end of the civil war.

117

Florence Parry Heide and Judith Heide C. Gilliland, *Sami and the Time of the Troubles.* New York: Clarion Books, 1992. An account of life during the civil war in Beirut told by a ten-year-old boy.

Siona Jenkins and Ann Jousiffe, *Lebanon.* Oakland: Lonely Planet, 2001. A newly updated and informative guidebook for the traveler. Includes interesting sections on history and culture and extensive maps and descriptions of the major areas of the country, including many historical sites.

Bernard Lewis, *The Middle East: A Brief History of the Last 2,000 Years.* New York: Scribner, 1996. A readable history of the many influences that have shaped the Middle East, including Christianity, Islam, and European imperialism.

Mario Pei, *The Story of Language.* New York: Meridian Books, 1984. A classic study of language by American linguist Mario Pei (1901–1978).

Kamal Salibi, A *House of Many Mansions: The History of Lebanon Reconsidered.* Berkeley: University of California Press, 1988. An analysis of Lebanese identity and history from different viewpoints.

———, *The Modern History of Lebanon.* New York: Caravan Books, 1996. An analysis of Lebanese social and political groups from the seventeenth century to approximately 1960.

Dorothy Stannard, ed., *Syria and Lebanon.* London: Insight Guides, 2000. A beautifully illustrated and informative travel guide to Lebanon and Syria. Extensive sections on history, people, and daily life.

PERIODICALS

Richard Covington, "Beirut Rises from the Ashes," *Smithsonian,* April 2000.

Sami G. Hajjar, "Creating Peace Between Lebanon and Israel," *Contemporary Review,* July, 2001.

Steven N. Simon and Jonathan Stevenson, "Declawing the Party of God: Toward Normalization in Lebanon," *World Policy Journal*, Summer 2001.

Internet Sources

Elizabeth Kassab, "The Paramount Reality of the Beirutis: War Literature and the Lebanese Conflict," *Lebanese Center for Policy Studies*. www.lcps-lebanon.org.

Farida Khizan, "Sculpture exhibit reaches for new heights," *Daily Star Online*, April 2000. www.dailystar.com.

Borre Ludvigsen, "Reflections on a Trip to Lebanon 1995," *Al Mashriq (The Levant)*. http://almashriq.hiof.no/lebanon.

Jean Said Makdisi, excerpts from *Beirut Fragments: A War Memoir, Al Mashriq (The Levant)*. http://almashriq.hiof.no/lebanon.

Marilyn Raschka, "Re-Rooting Lebanon's War-Displaced Farmers," *Washington Report on Middle East Affairs*, August/September 1997. www.washington-report.org.

Websites

CIA World Factbook 2001 (www.cia.gov). Statistical information about Lebanon, including geography, demographics, economy, transportation, government, and military.

Daily Star **Online** (www.dailystar.com). Online version of the daily newspaper with current news, feature stories, opinion pieces, and art, film, and book reviews.

Lebanese Center for Policy Studies (LCPS) (www.lcps-lebanon.org). A nonprofit research institute, LCPS publishes articles about political, social, and economic development in Lebanon.

al-Mashriq (the Levant) (http://almashriq.hiof.no/lebanon/) A repository of more than thirty-five thousand documents about culture and ways of life in Lebanon and the Levant. Maintained in Norway by Borre Ludvigsen who grew up in Lebanon.

UNRWA (www.un.org/unrwa/). Home page of the United Nations Relief and Works Agency for Palestine Refugees. Extensive statistical information about the 5 million Palestinian refugees in the Middle East, including camp and settlement locations in Lebanon.

Washington Report on Middle East Affairs (www.washington-report.org). Articles about current political and social events in the Middle East.

INDEX

Picture Credits

Cover Photo: © Roger Wood/CORBIS

© AFP/CORBIS, 16, 80

© Paul Almasy/CORBIS, 37

© Associated Press, AP, 27, 53, 55, 56, 61

© Associated Press, Jerome Delay, 65

© Associated Press, Hussein Malla, 78

© Associated Press, Ali Mohamed, 95, 103

© Associated Press, Saleh Rifai, 81

© Associated Press, Mahmoud Tawil, 66, 76, 88

© Associated Press, Mohamed Zatari, 73

© Getty Images, 63

© Hulton/Archive by Getty Images, 12, 46, 49, 50, 52

© Courtney Kealy/Liaison/Getty Images, 7, 70, 82, 92, 101

© Erich Lessing/Art Resource, NY, 30

Library of Congress, 86

© Francoise de Mulder/CORBIS, 23, 69

North Wind Picture Archives, 20

© Scott Peterson/Liaison/Getty Images, 93

© Reuters NewMedia, Inc./CORBIS, 21

© Reza/Webistan/CORBIS, 100

© Roger_Viollet/Getty Images, 42

© Roger Wood/CORBIS, 14

About the Author

Linda Hutchison lives in San Diego, California, and is a freelance writer. She has a bachelor's degree in communications from California State University Dominguez Hills.